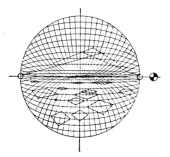

To Read Malb

perspective

a new system for designers   by Jay Doblin

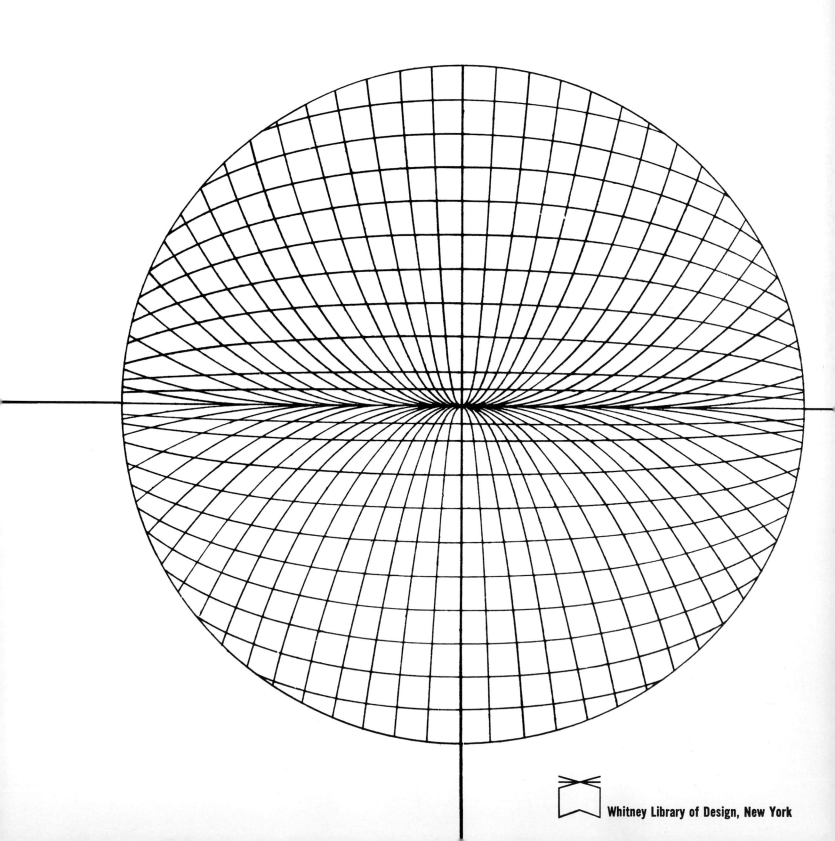

Whitney Library of Design, New York

Published by Whitney Library of Design
18 East 50th Street, New York, N. Y. 10022
© 1956 by Whitney Publications, Inc.

First printing 1956
Second printing 1958
Third printing 1961
Fourth printing 1963
Fifth printing 1966
Sixth printing 1968
Seventh printing 1969
Eighth printing 1970

Contents

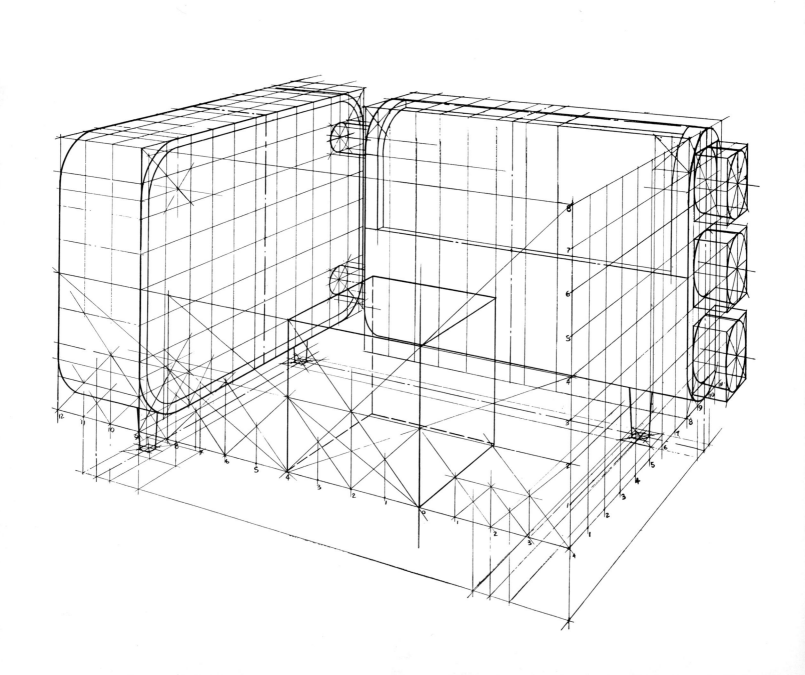

Introduction

The serious designer, faced with the problem of solidifying and transmitting design ideas, finds no single tool more effective—or more economical—than skill in perspective drawing. But it is an unwieldy tool, for the traditional methods of drawing in perspective are complicated and time-consuming. What is more important, they often result in inaccurate drawings.

These traditional systems were developed largely from the needs of the architect, who generally develops his ideas in plan, projecting drawings from the plan when his design is completed. A plan view of a tumbler or a juke box is obviously not very informative, however. The industrial designer must work out his ideas in the round, and although he can work with models or mock-ups, this is slow and costly. For him, perspective is not simply a means of communication but a working tool as indispensable as the architect's plans. He wants a simple method of creating on a two dimensional surface an accurate illusion of a three-dimensional object—a system that does not depend on plan views or elaborate constructions.

Generally speaking, there are two ways of drawing in perspective. One depends on the trained eye to judge convergence, depth, etc., and is usually called free-hand drawing, although drafting instruments may be used. The other involves the use of one of the constructional systems, and is commonly referred to as mechanical perspective.

During the four years that I served as chairman of the Evening School of Industrial Design at Pratt Institute I became increasingly dissatisfied with the two methods in general and the mechanical systems in particular. Both are important, and both were taught in the Evening School, but we began with the free-hand system because the over-all training was intended to sharpen the students' vision in preparation for design work.

We found that the free-hand system served the gifted students well but that their temperaments, when exposed to the tedium of the mechanical systems, often prevented them from making accurate drawings. The less talented students, who were unable to draw perspectives by eye, made poor mechanical perspectives because the systems themselves were deficient. Moreover, the mechanical systems did nothing to encourage their free-hand skill. This is not, unfortunately, just a student problem; similar difficulties arise in professional offices.

Badly drawn perspectives are almost without exception the result of three fundamental errors, all of which are inherent in the traditional perspective systems:

1. The angle of vision may exceed the limits of accurate drawing.

2. Because the systems are complex and tedious, the margin of error in the final drawing is multiplied.

3. The designer often fails to predict accurately the view, size, or scale of the drawing.

The number of perspective views that can be drawn of a single object is, of course, infinite, varying with each position of the observer. Most perspective systems are based on unlimited cases of perspective, but the one I will present is based on just three technical relationships of the observer and the object. It has unlimited applications, however: by using these three situations with their few clear rules, it is possible to draw any perspective view with the basic drafting instruments. The system has these important advantages:

1. It results in photographic accuracy.

2. It allows easy predetermination of the view, scale, and size of the drawing.

3. It encourages free-hand skill.

Any perspective system looks complicated in print. I suggest that you try this new system at your drafting board to see how simple it is.

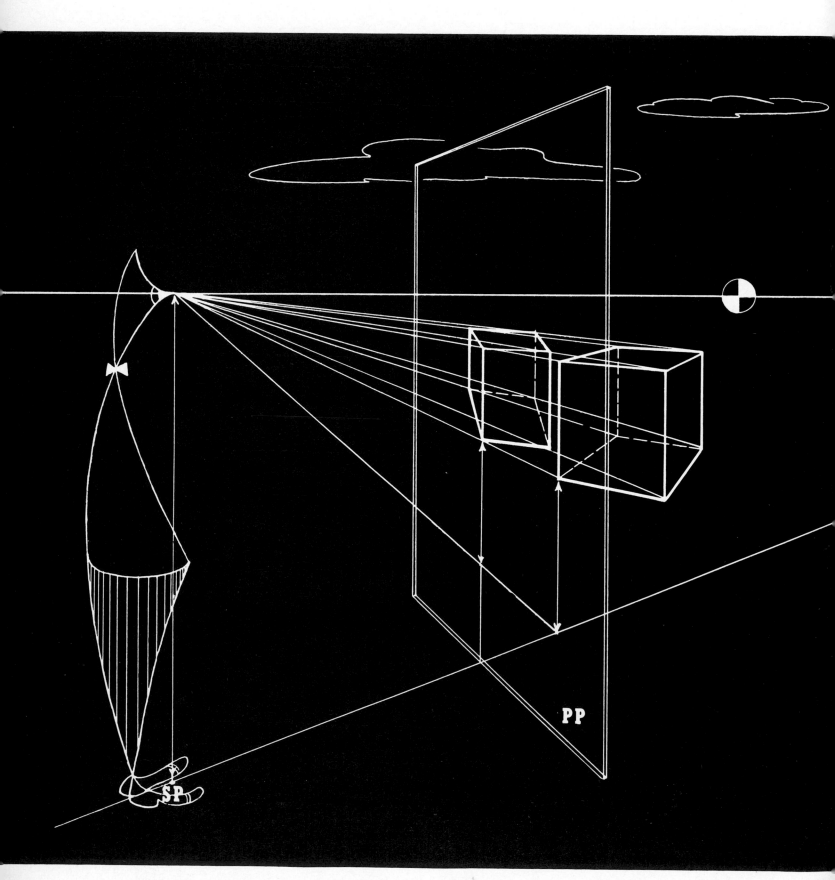

The basic principles of linear perspective

We are all aware of the way objects appear
to diminish and converge as their distance
from us increases. Stated simply, perspective
drawing is a way of reproducing this appearance of reality on a flat plane. Since we know
that objects do not really diminish and can
readily understand drawings in which they
maintain their true proportions, practical
perspective might be described as a way of
introducing systematic distortions into
drawings.

There are various methods of drawing in perspective, but all of them are based on the
same underlying principles:
1. A perspective drawing creates the illusion
of reality by relating the *observer*, the *object*,
and the *picture plane*.
2. The observer stands in a fixed position and
sees with one eye, like a camera. The position
of the eye is called the *station point*.
3. The surface on which the drawing is made
is called the *picture plane*, and is assumed
to be a plane placed between the observer and
the object at right angles to the observer's
line of sight. Lines drawn between
the object and the observer's eye will
intersect the picture plane at various points.
A perspective drawing is made by plotting
these points and connecting them. This is easy
to do if the picture plane is a piece of glass;
then the lines between the observer and the
object are rays of light; the image on the
glass is a perspective view and can be
traced directly. Usually, however, the picture
plane is a piece of paper on a drafting
board, and the perspective drawing must be
projected on it by one of the perspective
systems or visualized and sketched free hand.
4. The horizon is assumed to be at an
infinite distance from the observer, so that
parallel lines meet at the horizon and
objects on the horizon appear to be points.
These points are called *vanishing points*.
5. Although in perspective drawing we are
concerned with the diminishing of objects,
for convenience we break these objects into
lines and planes and study the way the lines
and planes diminish.
6. The *cube* is the basic form in perspective,
and will be used as the object throughout
most of the text, because it can be used as
a perspective unit to measure height, width,
and depth concurrently. Theoretically, the
perspective cube can be multiplied and divided
into any combination of height, width, and
depth to provide a basis for drawing any object.

Current texts set forth three basic working
methods for constructing perspective drawings.
Before proceeding to the new system, it will
be helpful to review these three traditional
systems. I shall not present a complete de-
scription of them, but simply show how they
are used to erect a basic perspective cube.
These systems are all accurate for drawing the
cube; they admit inaccuracies as the scope of
the drawing increases.

The two elevation system

The perspective drawing is derived from two orthographic drawings, a top view and a side view, which must be projected through two picture planes toward two observers.

Advantage: The system is useful if top and side views have already been made.

Disadvantages: The amount of drawing is time-consuming and conducive to error and confusion. If the station points are remote the construction will be unwieldy. The vanishing points cannot be located until the drawing is completed. Size, view, and scale are difficult to foresee. When orthographic drawings exist, the side view must usually be redrawn at the proper rotation. If drawings do not exist, the labor required is prohibitive.

The top plan system

The top plan system is easier to understand and faster because it requires only a top view and vanishing points.

Advantages: The system is useful if a plan view has already been made. It is less complex than the two elevation system and easier to visualize. It uses an actual-scale height measurement. It provides the vanishing points immediately.

Disadvantages: The location of a station point and long parallels can be cumbersome.

The measuring point system

The sides of the cube are derived from vanishing points; the depth of the cube is established by the use of measuring points, which are actually the vanishing points of lines relative to the cube.

Advantages: No plans or elevations are necessary. The cube is easily multiplied directly from the basic construction.

Disadvantages: The theory is complex (below). Construction of the station points and large right angle is cumbersome.

To locate the measuring points of a cube

1. Draw a top view *abcd* of the cube and place it against the horizon at *d*.
2. Drop a vertical at *d* and locate *SP*.
3. Draw parallels to the sides of the cube from *SP* to locate *VP-L* and *VP-R*.
4. Measuring points *MP-A* and *MP-B* can be located as follows: Rotate point *a* from *d* to the horizon, locating point *A*; draw a line from *A* through *a*; draw a parallel to *Aa* from *SP* to the horizon, locating *MP-A*; this is the vanishing point of line *Aa*. Repeat for point *b*, locating *MP-B*. Since *Ada* and *VP-L* are equal angles because their sides are parallel, we can find *MP-A* and *MP-B* simply by rotating *SP* from *VP-L* and *VP-R*.
5. Find the nearest angle *n* of the cube by measuring any desired distance from *d*.
6. Draw perspective lines from *n* to construct the nearest angle.
7. Draw a measuring line horizontally through *n*.
8. Mark the length of the cube side on either side of *n*, locating *x*, and *y*.
9. Draw the line *Aa* in perspective by connecting *x* with *MP-A*. Where this line intersects the line from *n* a corner of the cube will appear. Repeat for *Bb*. We now have all the points necessary to complete the cube.

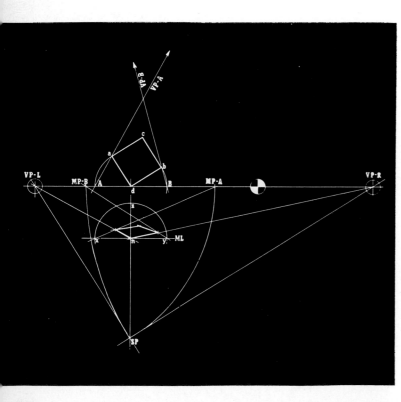

To draw a cube using the two elevation system:

1. Draw a top view T of the cube and place it against the picture plane at x.
2. Locate a station point SP-T by dropping a perpendicular at x and scaling off any desired distance in relation to the cube size.
3. Connect SP-T to all important points on T and note their intersections with the picture plane.
4. Draw a side view S of the cube and place it against a side view of the picture plane.
5. Locate eye level y by measuring any desired distance along the side view picture plane from the top (x) of S.
6. Locate the side view station point SP-S by drawing a line horizontally from y equal to the distance between SP-T and the top view picture plane.
7. Connect SP-S to all important points on S and note their intersections with the picture plane.
8. Drop all points on the top view picture plane.
9. Extend all points on the side view picture plane horizontally.
10. Cross-reference all points on the grid formed between the top and side views of the cube (note cross-referencing of points A to locate A in perspective) and connect them properly to form cube.

To draw a cube using the top plan system:

1. Draw a horizontal line to serve dually as horizon and picture plane.
2. Draw a top view of the cube at any angle with nearest corner touching the picture plane at x.
3. Locate the station point SP by dropping a perpendicular from the horizon at x and scaling off any desired distance in relation to cube size.
4. From SP draw lines a and b parallel to sides A and B to intersect the horizon at vp-l and vp-r. These points are the vanishing points.
5. Connect SP with all important points of the cube and note the intersections at the picture plane (1, 2, and 3).
6. Drop verticals from 1, 2, and 3.
7. The distance of the perspective cube from eye level is laid off on SP-x, locating the nearest angle N of the cube. xN cannot exceed SP-x.
8. Lay off the height of the cube from N toward x.
9. Draw perspective lines from the bottom and top of the cube height to vp-l and vp-r.
10. At the intersections of the perspective lines and the verticals draw the remaining perspective lines to complete the cube.

To draw a cube using the measuring point system:

1. Draw a horizon.
2. Set up two vanishing points vp-L and vp-R.
3. Drop a vertical from any point on the horizon, depending on the view desired.
4. Construct a right triangle with the distance between vp-L and vp-R as its hypotenuse and its apex on the vertical locating station point SP.
5. Divide the vertical to any scale according to the distance of the observer from the object and place the nearest angle N at any desired distance from eye level.
6. Draw measuring line ml horizontally through N.
7. Lay off the true height of the cube from N to z and rotate it to the measuring line, locating x and y.
8. Draw perspective lines to N, forming the nearest angle of the cube.
9. Locate measuring points mp-Y and mp-X by rotating SP from vp-L and vp-R.
10. Connect mp-X to x and note its intersection with the perspective line from N.
11. Repeat for mp-Y and y.
12. Draw verticals at the intersections and complete cube by drawing the remaining perspective lines.

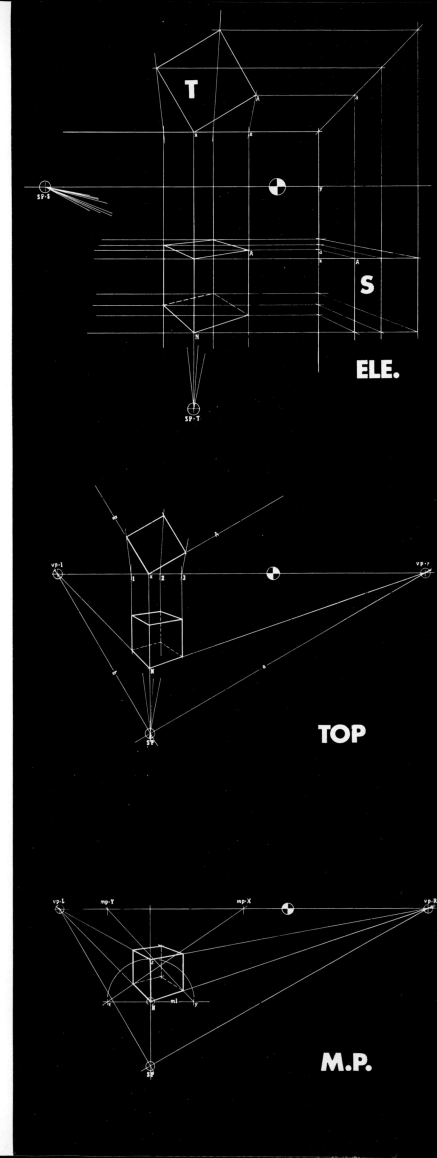

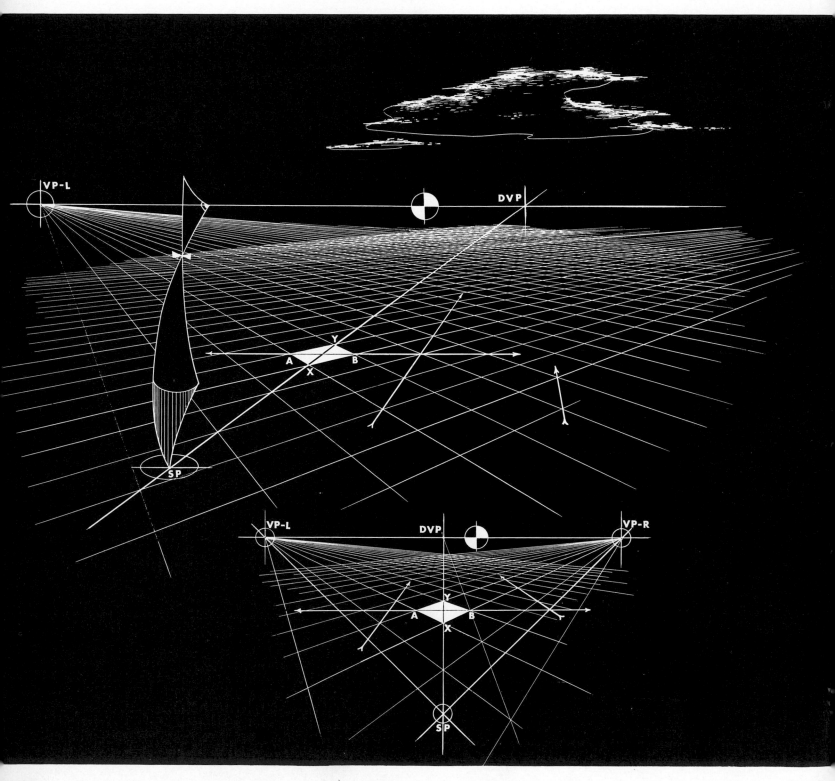

The traditional systems we have just reviewed give general rules that can be used to develop any perspective view. However, in the opening section it was mentioned that an accurately constructed cube can theoretically be multiplied and divided indefinitely. This means that if we can find any views of the cube that are particularly easy to draw, we should be able to multiply these basic cubes to provide cubes at every angle to the observer.

The simplest view of the cube is the 45° oblique view. Because this view is easy to construct and lends itself to the development of additional information, it will be used as a starting point for our discussion.

45° oblique perspective

To understand 45° oblique perspective, examine the case of an observer standing on a tile floor that extends to the horizon in every direction. He cannot see all of this vista at once. If he turns so that his line of sight is at an angle of 45° to the sides of the tiles, he will notice several things:

1. The diagonals of all the tiles within his range of vision seem to meet at a single point on the horizon directly in front of him. This point will be called the *diagonal vanishing point* or *DVP*.

2. The sides of the tiles converge at equal angles to the right and left toward their respective vanishing points (*VP-L* and *VP-R*).

3. If he examines one tile directly in his line of sight (*AXBY*) he sees that the side to side diagonal (*AB*) is horizontal and parallel to the horizon. This fact is extremely important to our system. Proof of it is given below.

Proof that the diagonal of the square in 45° oblique perspective is horizontal

Given the triangle *LnR*, in which RL is bisected at *D* by *nD; nL* is intersected at *a* by *Ra; Rn* is intersected at *b* by *Lb; Ra* and *Lb* intersect each other at *c* on *nD;*

To prove that *ab* is parallel to *LR*:

1. Extend *nD* and mark off *DZ* equal to *Dc*.

2. Since *RD* equals *LD* and *DZ* equals *Dc* and we know that the diagonals of a parallelogram bisect each other, *RLcZ* is a parallelogram.

3. Since *bc* and *RZ* are parallel, they divide the angle *RnZ* in the same ratio and *nb/bR* equals *nc/cZ*.

4. Similarly, since *ac* and *LZ* are parallel lines, they divide angle *LnZ* in the same ratio, and *nc/cZ* equals *na/aL*.

5. Therefore *nb/bR* equals *na/aL*, and since lines *nR* and *nL* are divided in the same ratio, the segments mark off parallel lines.

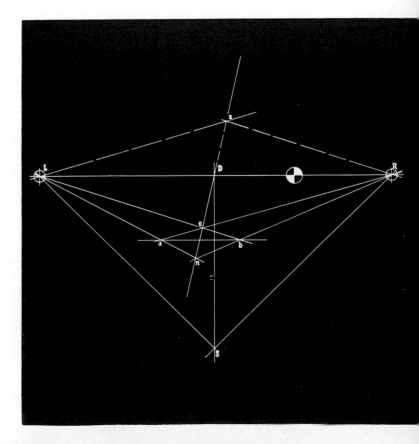

Construction of a cube in 45° perspective

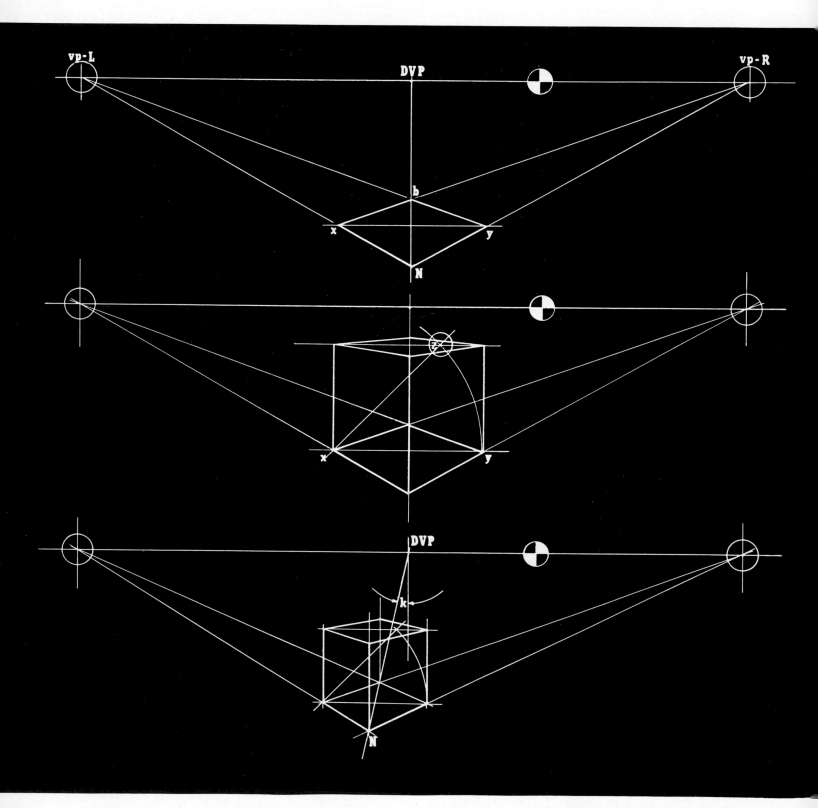

Since the diagonal of the square in 45° oblique perspective is parallel to the horizon and the picture plane it has no convergence.
Thus it provides a constant measure which can be used to erect a cube.

Construction of the diagonal plane of a cube in 45° oblique perspective

To construct the diagonal plane of a cube, given the horizontal diagonal xy:
1. Erect the verticals at x and y.
2. Draw a diagonal line at 45° from x.
3. Rotate point y from x until it intersects the diagonal, locating point z.
4. Draw a horizontal through z.
Since xz equals xy, $axwz$ is a side of the cube whose diagonal equals xy, and $axyb$ is the diagonal plane of that cube.

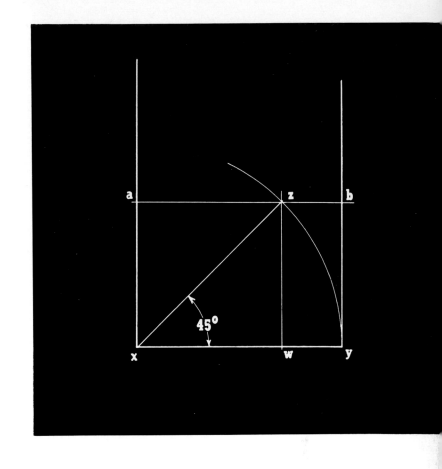

Construction of a cube in 45° oblique perspective

To create a horizontal square in 45° oblique perspective, we need only apply the conditions observed in the diagram on the preceding page.
1. Draw a horizon and place two vanishing points vp-L and vp-R on it.
2. Bisect the distance between vanishing points to locate diagonal vanishing point DVP.
3. Drop a perpendicular or near perpendicular from DVP. This line is a diagonal of the square.
4. Draw two lines from vp-L and vp-R to intersect at the desired angle on the diagonal. This gives the nearest angle N of the square.
5. Draw two more perspective lines to intersect on the diagonal at the desired distance above N, enclosing the figure $xybN$.
$zybN$ is a horizontal square because it fulfills the visual conditions given on the preceding page: a) The diagonal goes to DVP, which is half way between vp-R and vp-L. b) Front and rear corners lie on the diagonal. c) The side to side diagonal is truly horizontal (proof on previous page). d) The four sides converge to their respective vanishing points.
We can easily complete the cube by erecting a diagonal plane on this square:
6. Erect verticals at all four corners of the square.
7. Construct the diagonal plane of the cube by rotating point y 45° upward to point z and drawing a horizontal through point z to intersect the side verticals (proof above).
8. Construct the upper square of the cube by drawing perspective lines through intersections.

This cube is absolutely accurate and can be checked against any constructional system. It is constructed directly from the horizon, without station points, elevations, long parallels or angles, measuring points, etc. Since the front to back diagonal need not be vertical so long as it goes to the DVP (previous page), we have established a simple method of drawing an accurate cube in a variety of positions.
However, distortion will occur if the diagonal is too far from the vertical. On the basis of traditional perspective theory, there is no explanation for this distortion.

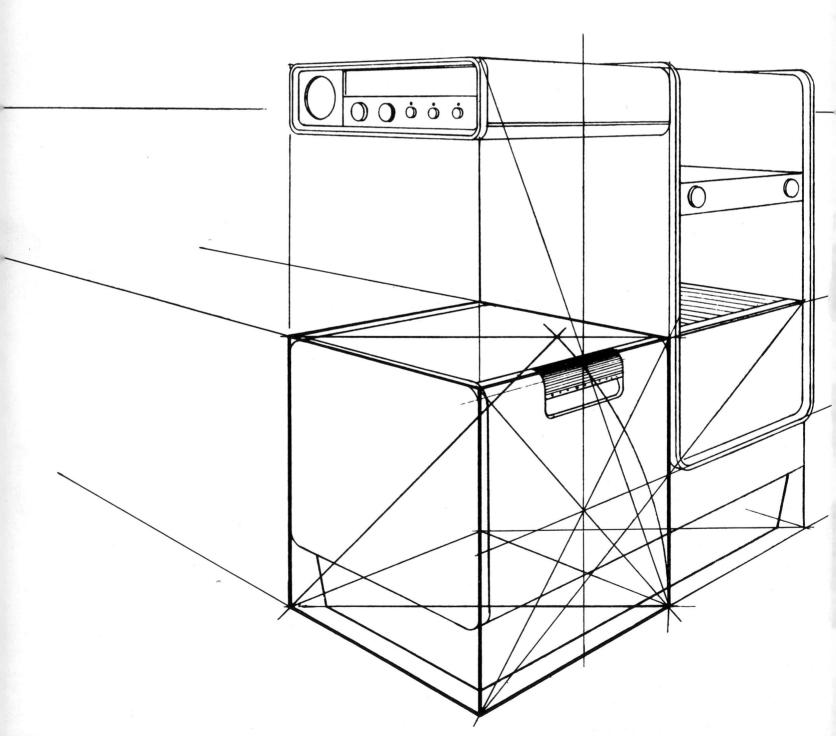

This drawing of a range is based on a 45° view of the cube. The basic form, achieved by multiplication, is twice as high and twice as wide as the original cube. The 45° view is especially appropriate for an object with two interesting sides because it shows both sides with equal emphasis. Since the width of the range is greater than its depth, the view is not monotonous, but if the range were symmetrical another view would probably be more interesting.

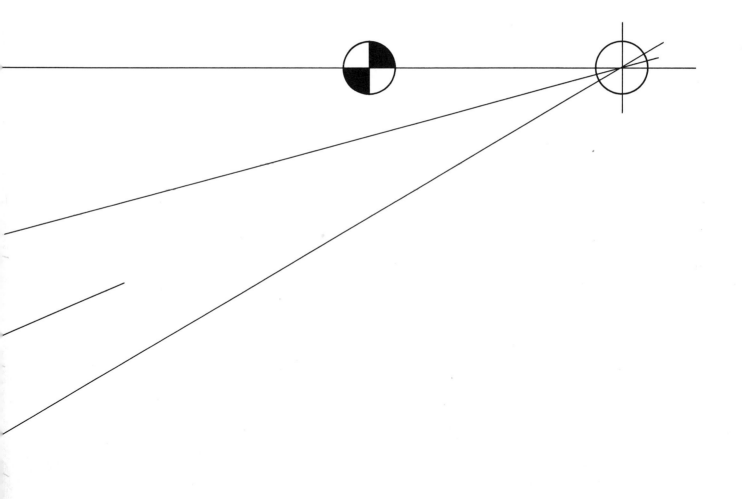

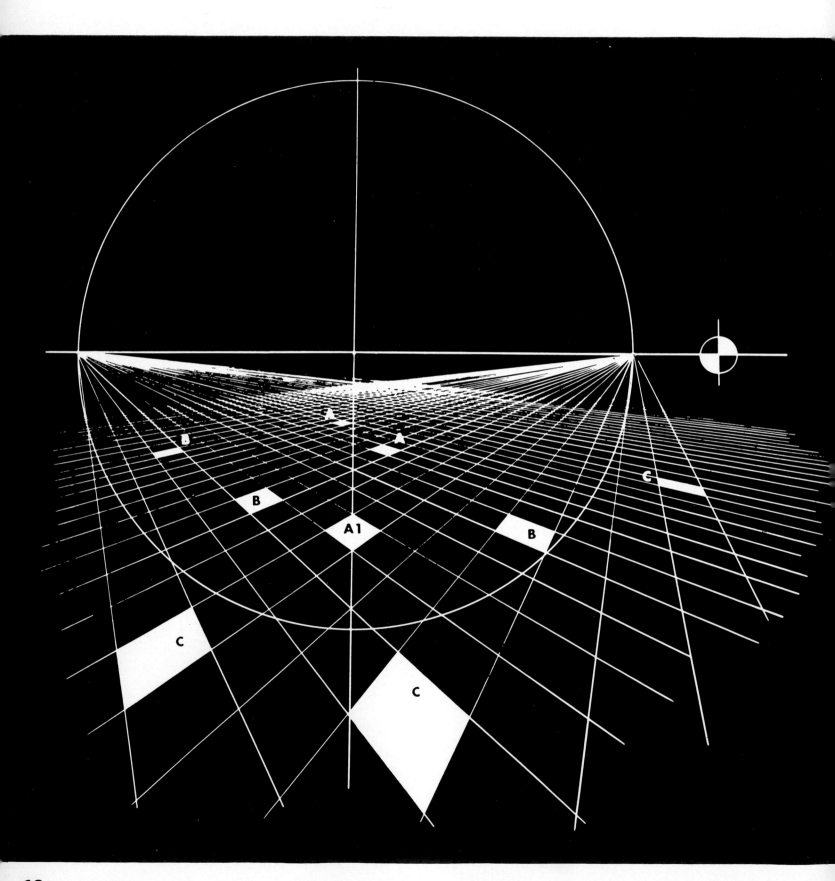

In the last chapter we discovered a simple method for erecting a cube in 45° oblique perspective. According to traditional theory, we should be able to multiply this cube in any direction and use it as a basis for constructing any figure. To see if this is true, draw a horizontal square in 45° oblique perspective (A1) and project it into a complete vista of horizontal squares. Now examine a few random squares and notice how many look distorted. These distortions result from two types of error, which we must learn to avoid if we want to make correct drawings. The first error is fairly simple, and most draftsmen know how to control it. The second is more complicated. To my knowledge it has never been described.

Control of the nearest angle

If an observer looks at a book held horizontally at eye level, the nearest angle is 180°— a straight line. As he lowers the book the nearest angle becomes more acute until it finally reaches 90°. When this happens, the book is at right angles to his line of sight and he is seeing it in plan. It is obviously impossible for a plan view to occur in a horizontal vista; thus it is impossible for any square in true perspective to have a nearest angle of 90°. Any square in a perspective vista whose nearest angle is 90° or less is distorted.
A simple way of imposing this limitation is to swing a circle from the horizon to intersect the vanishing points. We know from geometry that any angle formed on the perimeter of a circle by lines from the intersections of the circle and its diameter will be a right triangle. Thus any nearest angle that touches the circle will be distorted; any nearest angle within the circle will be greater than 90°.

Side to side error

We have now eliminated the kind of distortion found in squares C, but if we examine our vista again we find many squares inside the circle look distorted. Those marked A look all right, but those marked B look increasingly distorted as their horizontal distance from the original square increases. We can check the accuracy of some of these squares by comparing them with squares drawn individually by the top plan method, which we know is accurate for drawing individual squares.

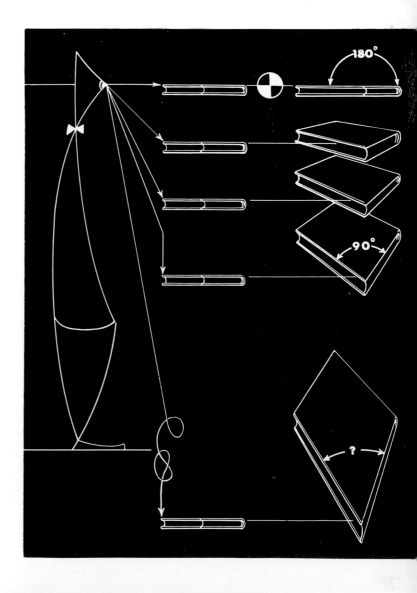

Comparison of correct squares with grid squares

In order to draw the top-plan squares that correspond with our grid squares, we must have an accurate plan view of each square. Ordinarily, when we use the top-plan method, we start with a plan view and find the vanishing points when the perspective view is completed. But in this case, since we already know the vanishing points, we must work backwards from them to find the correct plan view. This is done as follows: Draw a perpendicular through the nearest angle of grid squares A,B, and C and locate the station point at the intersection of this perpendicular with a circle drawn through the vanishing points. Make a right angle at the station point by drawing lines to the vanishing points. Draw the nearest angle of the plan view square at the horizon with its sides parallel to the right angle. We are not particularly concerned with the size of the plan view squares; a convenient width can be found by projecting the next nearest angle of each grid square through the horizon. Now complete the plan-view squares and project them through the horizon to produce correct perspective squares over grid squares A,B, and C.

When we check squares A, B, and C against the corresponding top-plan squares we find that B and C accumulate error as they move away from the original, A. The nearest angles in each pair of squares coincide, and the sides are parallel; the significant difference is in the diagonals. Notice how diagonals 1, 2, and 3 change angle as they approach the vanishing point—in other words, the squares rotate as they move between the vanishing points.

Curved diagonals

Using the top-plan method, let us construct a series of horizontal squares across the circle of correct drawing and line them up along their diagonals. We find that the diagonals generate a curve. If we draw hundreds of accurate horizontal squares and line up their diagonals, the diagonals will make a figure like that at the bottom of the opposite page. A perfectly accurate drawing of any horizontal square in two-point perspective can be made on this figure simply by connecting perspective lines from the vanishing points so that they intersect on the diagonals.

The implications of this figure are startling: In a perfectly accurate perspective drawing, the only straight lines will be those that cross the observer's line of sight. This may seem remarkable at first, but we can see it is so by the evidence of our eyes. Consider the case of an observer looking at a long low building at right angles to his line of sight. The building will appear largest where it crosses his line of sight. At the sides of the vista it is further from him and will therefore appear to diminish. The roof, if it is above his line of sight, will curve down toward the horizon; the bottom, if it is below his line of sight, will appear to curve upward. Only if one of these lines is directly at eye level will it appear to be straight.

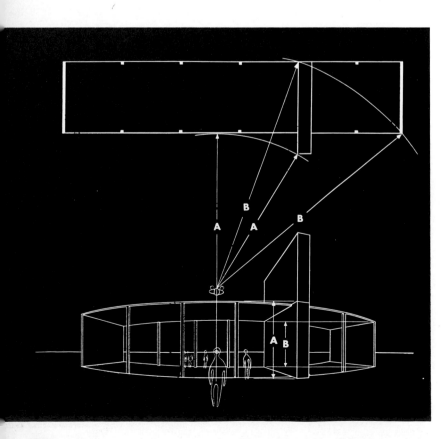

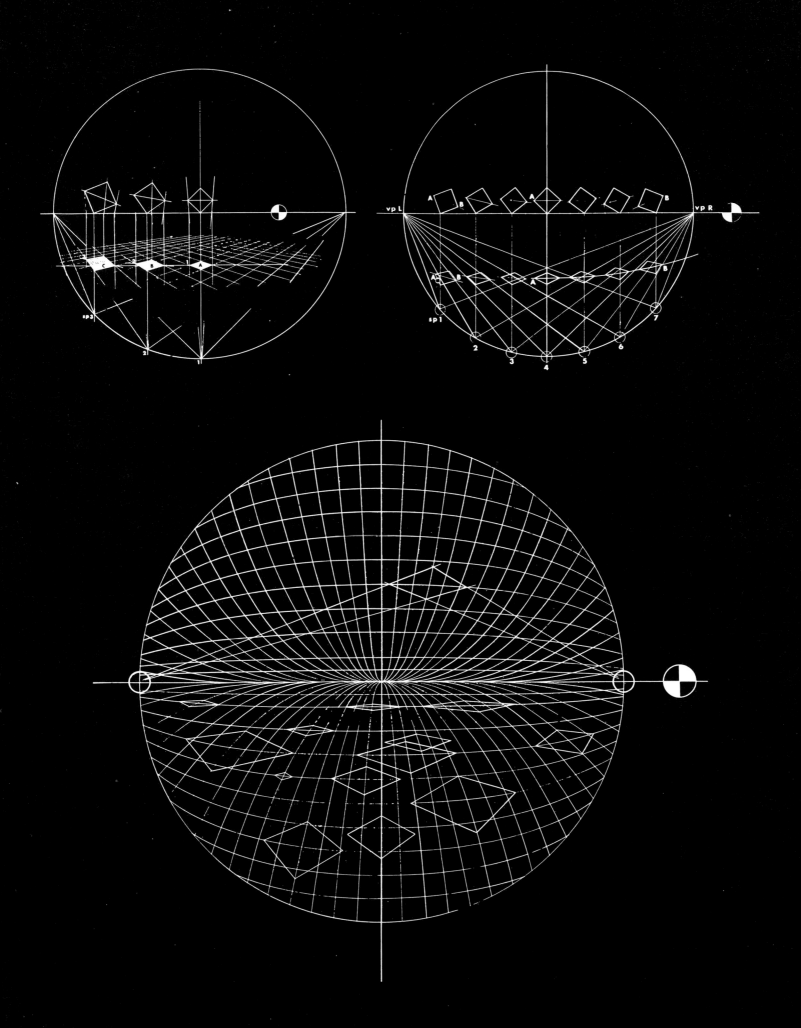

ERR   The control of error

It will help us to deal with error if we understand that accuracy is a relative thing in perspective. A drawing is a flat plane, and the eye registers impressions on a tiny, curved surface. Furthermore, perspective drawing is based on the assumption that the observer views any scene with one unmoving eye. It is true that the eye has a remarkably wide angle of vision: with both eyes looking straight ahead we can see almost a full 180°. But it would be difficult to draw what we see in this way. We gain an accurate impression of such a vista by moving our eyes constantly to look at each part directly. In the language of perspective, we see one scene with many horizons and vanishing points. Perspective drawing will always remain a system for *symbolizing* what the eye sees. Our aim is to make drawings that look accurate by learning to control the inevitable error.

Tolerable error

It would certainly be almost impossible to draw rectangular objects with curved lines, and our habits of seeing would make such a drawing look absurd. The curvilinear grid on the preceding page is not useful in drawing, but it does show us how distortion multiplies as side-to-side vista increases. We can apply this knowledge in two ways. If we are drawing a broad vista, we know we will have to tolerate some error, but we can learn to keep it within reasonable limits. If we are drawing a single object by developing an easily constructed view of the cube — and that is the basis of the system outlined in this book — we must find how far the cube can be extended before the error becomes intolerable. We saw on the previous page how a cube rotates on its diagonal according to its position between the vanishing points. If we wish to draw a cube at 45° to the observer, we must draw it half way between the vanishing points. The same construction can be used to draw a cube slightly to one side of center, but if the cube is considerably off center, the error in the diagonal begins to show up.

By comparing correct squares with grid squares, as we did on the preceding page, it is possible to determine the exact percentage of error that occurs at any point on a vista created by multiplying one square. At the right are two scales, one showing how error accrues in a vista developed from the 45° oblique view of a square, the other showing the error in a vista developed from a square correctly drawn at the 30-60° rotation. In order to find out how much error the trained eye could tolerate, I presented a test made up of correct and incorrect cubes to a large group of professional designers (left). I discovered that visual accord is assured if the error in depth does not exceed 25 percent. The 45° scale at right shows that an error of 25 percent occurs about half way to the vanishing points. In other words, the method presented for drawing a 45° view of the cube can be used to draw a cube at any rotation from the center half way to the vanishing points. At this point the error becomes intolerable and we need a view that is acceptable at the sides of the vista. Such a view is the 30-60° rotation.

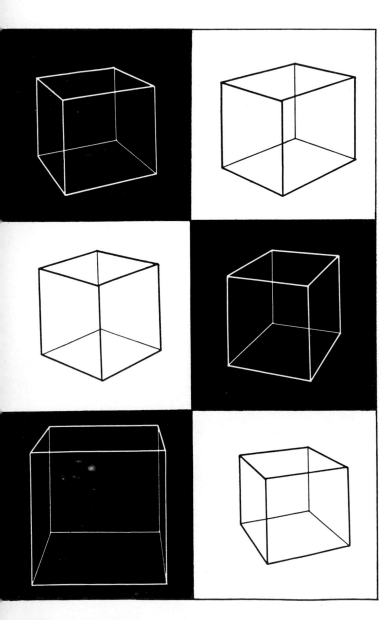

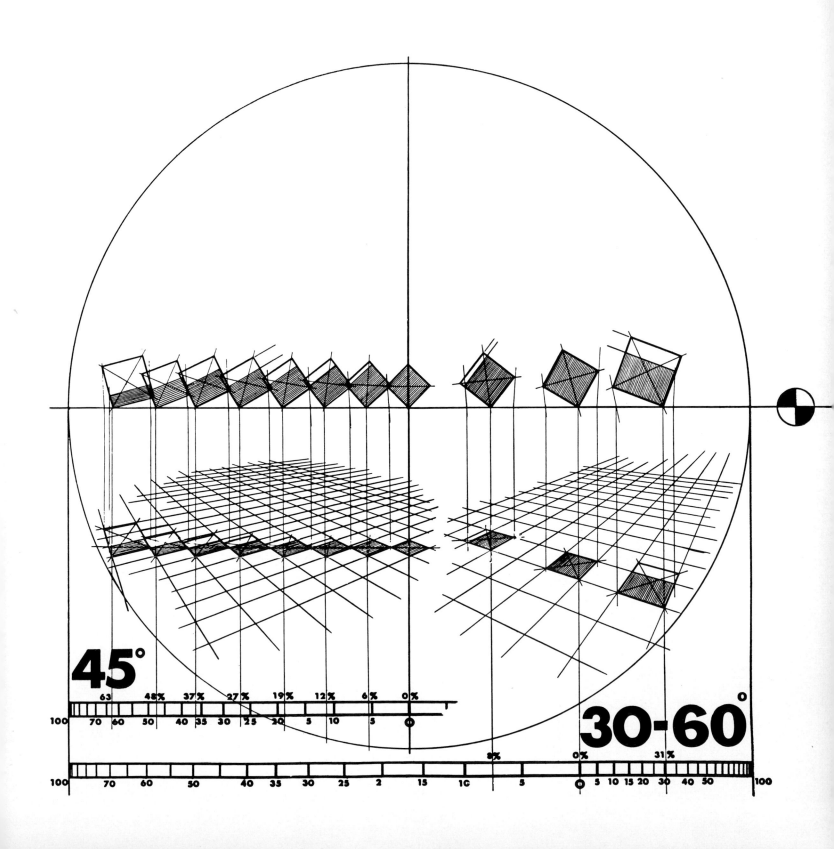

45°

63 48% 37% 27% 19% 12% 6% 0%

100 70 60 50 40 35 30 25 20 5 10 5 0

30-60°

8% 0% 31%

100 70 60 50 40 35 30 25 2 15 10 5 0 5 10 15 20 30 40 50 100

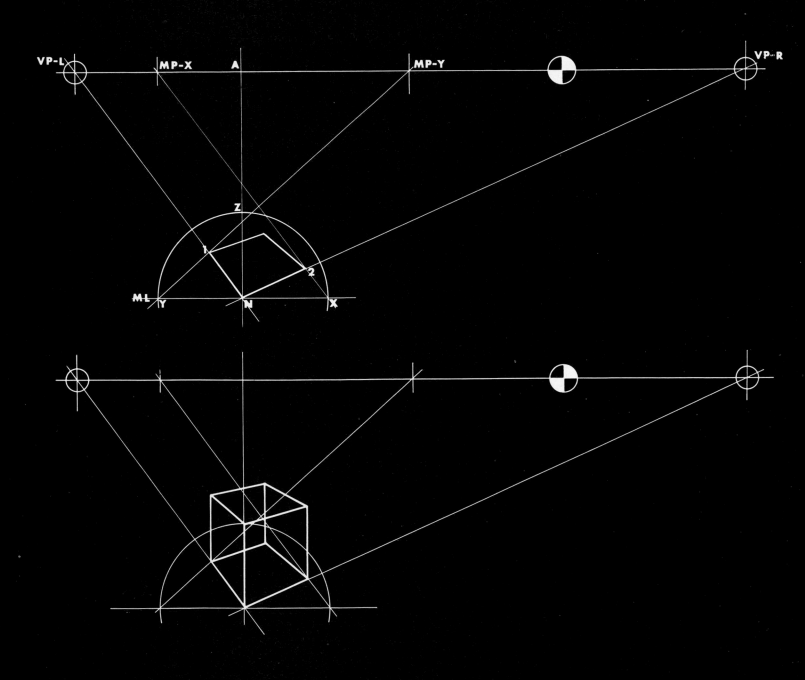

Special case of 30-60° measuring points

Ordinarily, drawing a 30-60° view of the cube by the measuring point system requires the following preliminary construction: Draw a horizon and place two vanishing points on it (L and R); using L-R as the hypotenuse, construct a 30-60° right triangle with the apex at S; draw a vertical from S intersecting the horizon at A; rotate S to the horizon from L and R to locate the measuring points X and Y. At the 30-60° rotation it happens that the measuring points X and Y and the vertical at A can be located without construction of a right angle, by simple division of the hypotenuse (LR).

We know that the short side of a 30-60° triangle equals half the hypotenuse; thus in LSR LR equals $2LS$, and since LS equals LY, Y is the midpoint of LR.

In the 30-60° triangle LAS, LS equals $2LA$, and since LS equals LY, A is the midpoint of LY. We also know that the sum of the squares of the two sides of a right triangle equals the square of the hypotenuse; thus LS^2 plus RS^2 equals LR^2; and if LR equals 2, then LS equals 1; so that 1 plus RS^2 equals 4 and RS equals 1.732, and since RS equals RX, RX equals 1.732. For practical purposes, 1.732 becomes 1.750. Thus, if LR equals 2, RX equals 1¾.

In short, we can find Y by bisecting LR, A by bisecting LY, and X by bisecting LA.

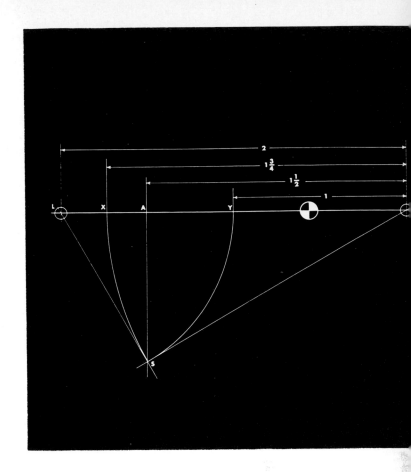

Construction of a 30-60° view of the cube

1.   Draw a horizon and establish two vanishing points VP-L and VP-R.
2.   Bisect the distance between the vanishing points to locate measuring point MP-Y.
3.   Bisect the distance between MP-Y and VP-L to locate A.
4.   Bisect the distance between A and VP-L to locate measuring point MP-X.
5.   Draw a vertical at A and place nearest angle N of the cube at the desired distance above or below eye level.
6.   Draw a horizontal measuring line (ML) through N.
7.   Lay off the height of the cube from N to Z and rotate Z to the measuring line, locating X and Y.
8.   Draw perspective lines to N to construct the nearest angle.
9.   Draw a line from MP-Y to Y and note its intersection with the perspective line at 1. Repeat for MP-Z and Z, locating 2.
10.   Draw perspective lines to the intersections at 1 and 2 to complete the horizontal square.
11.   Erect verticals at all corners of the square.
12.   Draw perspective lines to Z; complete the cube. This cube is absolutely accurate and may be checked by any other system. It supplements the 45° oblique view, allowing us to draw a cube at any rotation between the vanishing points with an error of less than 25 percent. The error exceeds 25 percent in the 30-60° cube when it crosses the center or approaches the vanishing points. When it reaches the vanishing points, there is 100 percent error, so a vanishing point can never properly be included in a two-point perspective.

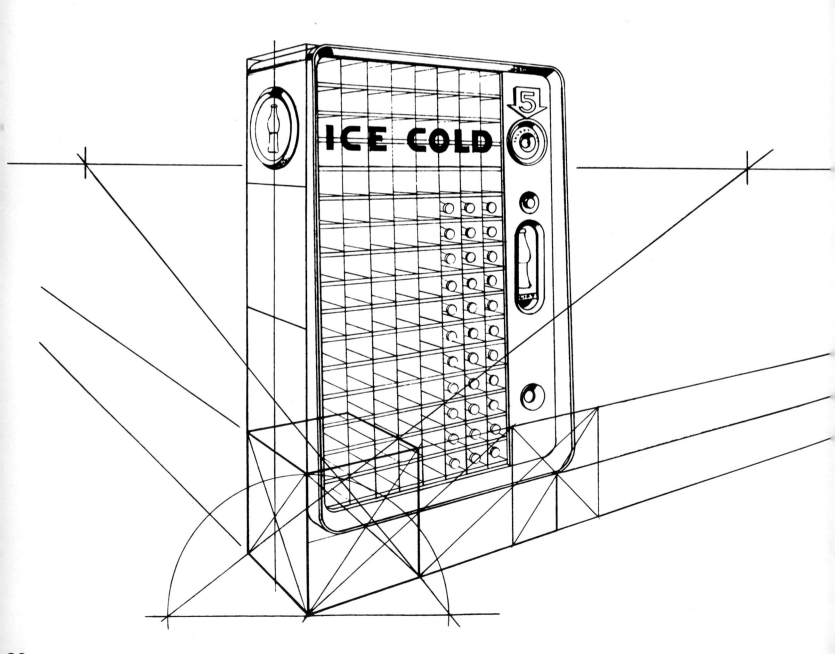

ICE COLD

This drawing of a dispensing machine was
developed from a 30-60° view of the cube. The
basic figure is four times as high and two and a
half times as wide as the original cube. In
practice, the final drawing would be made on
tracing paper over the original construction so
that no guide lines would appear. The 30-60°
view is particularly appropriate for an object
with one important side because it emphasizes
one side while still showing the depth of the
object and the configuration of a second side.
If the interior of the machine were more
important than the second side we would
presumably choose parallel perspective.

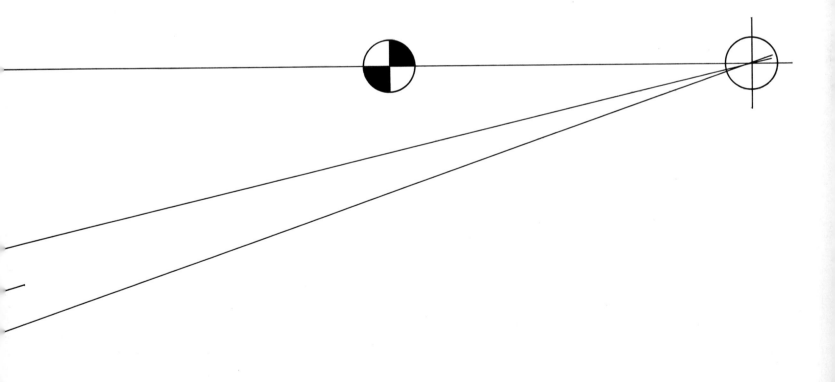

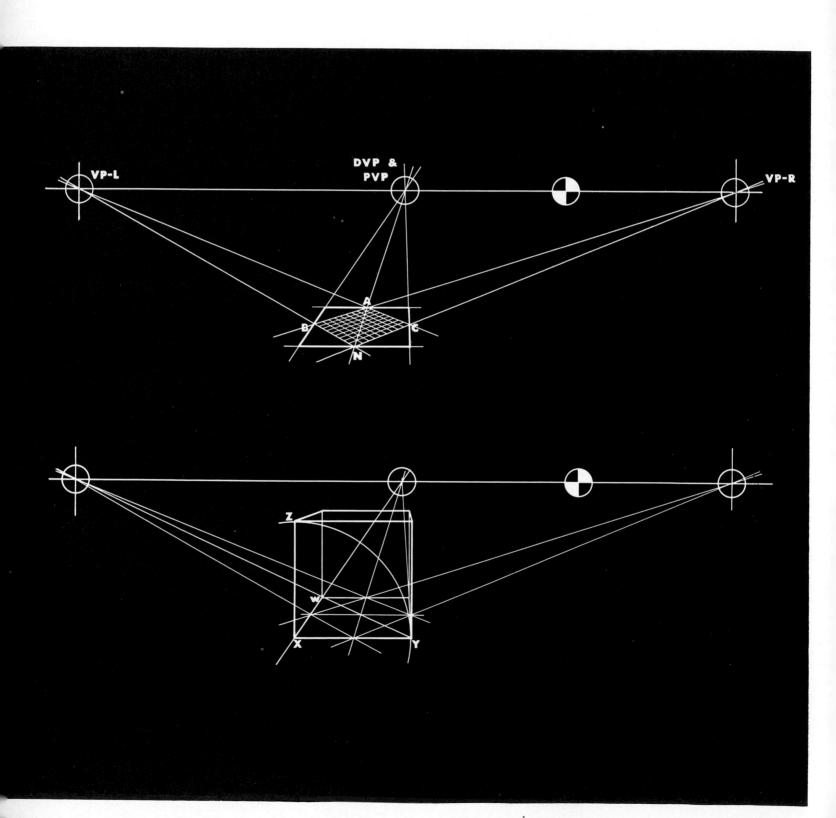

Parallel perspective

We now have simple methods for drawing two specific views of the cube — the 45° view and the 30-60° view. We know that one or the other of these methods can be used to draw any oblique perspective view of the cube. However, an oblique perspective view can never include a vanishing point. In some drawings, particularly street scenes and interiors, the inclusion of a vanishing point is desirable because it permits us to show three side planes of the cube from within. A view which includes one vanishing point (or which has one vanishing point above or below the picture rather than off to one side) is in one-point or parallel perspective. Although it is the oldest and simplest form of perspective, parallel perspective is still poorly understood. It can be regarded as a case of 45° perspective, for the two forms are interlocked. We can see this by re-examining the tile floor that was used to illustrate 45° perspective. If we study the diagonals of the tiles, we find that they form squares in parallel perspective. The diagonals fulfill two conditions: the vanishing point of the front-to-rear diagonals appears in the center of the drawing, and the side-to-side diagonals are truly parallel to the horizon. Since the 45° square is easily drawn directly from the vanishing points, we can use it as a quick guide for drawing a square in parallel perspective.

Construction of a square in parallel perspective
1. Draw a horizon and place two vanishing points *VP-L* and *VP-R* on it.
2. Bisect the distance between the vanishing points to locate the diagonal vanishing point *DVP*. This is also the parallel perspective vanishing point.
3. Draw perspective lines from *VP-L* and *VP-R* to create a horizontal square *BNCA*, making certain that the nearest angle *N* does not approach 90°.
4. Draw diagonals through *A* and *N* parallel to the horizon.
5. Draw diagonals through *C* and *B* to *DVP*. These four diagonals form a square in parallel perspective. If we examine our tile drawing again we see that it is not necessary to complete the 45° square in order to draw a square in parallel perspective. A line drawn from one vanishing point through the middle of the 45° square will be the diagonal of the square in parallel perspective and serve to establish its depth (right).

Construction of a cube in parallel perspective
1. Draw a horizon and place two vanishing points on it. Bisect the distance between them to find the diagonal vanishing point.
2. Draw the front edge *X-Y* of the cube parallel to the horizon and rotate it upward 90° to *Z* to find the height of the cube.
3. Draw a perspective line from *VP-L* to *Y*.
4. Draw a perspective line from *DVP* to *X* intersecting the line from *VP-L* at *W*.
5. Draw a horizontal through *W*. This is the rear edge of the cube.
6. Complete the cube.
Less side-to-side shift can be tolerated in parallel perspective than in 30-60° or 45° perspective. Care must be taken to prevent distortion at extremes of the drawing.

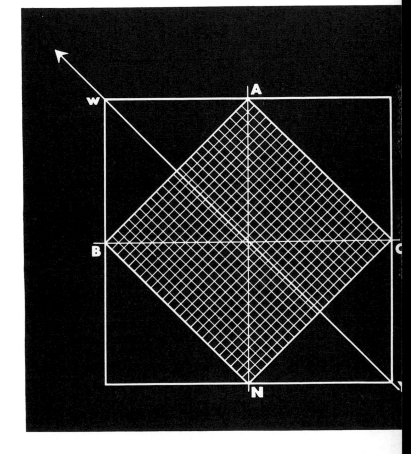

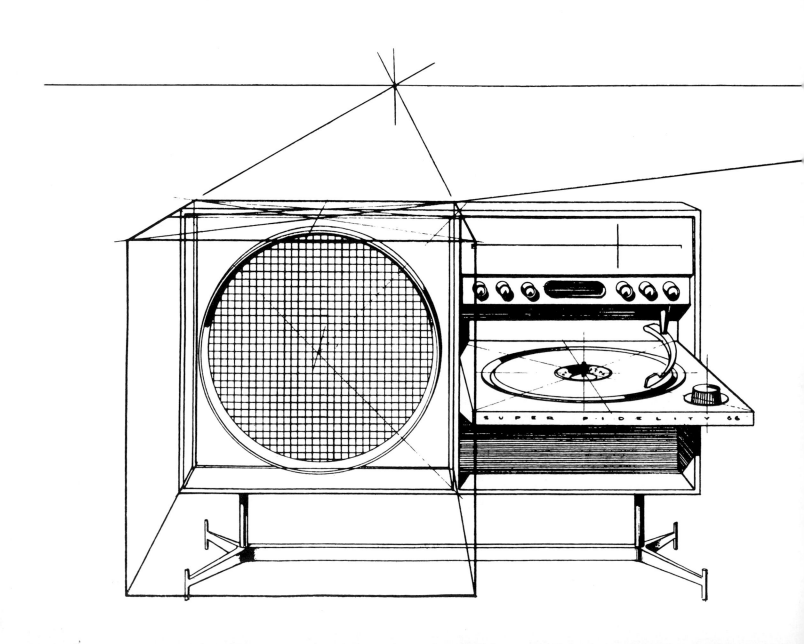

This drawing of a radio-phonograph was
developed from a cube in parallel perspective.
The largest possible cube was used to avoid the
distortion that crops up so easily in parallel
perspective: the basic box is twice the width and
less than half the depth of the original cube.
The parallel view was chosen because certain
details of the interior would have been lost from
any other angle, and the sides of the product
are uneventful. Parallel perspective does not
always give a clear indication of the depth of an
object, but in this case the depth is not hard to
judge: the size of the turntable is one clue.

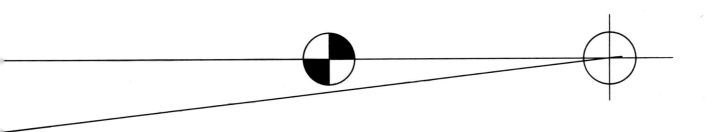

Before we begin a drawing we must settle three things: the view, the scale of the object, and the size of the drawing. View, or the angle of rotation of object to observer, has been our subject so far. We now have simple methods for drawing three perspective views of the cube. Each method can be used to produce a range of views, so that by choosing the proper method we can draw an accurate cube at any angle to the observer. The preliminary construction in each case is simply a horizon and two vanishing points.

The 45° view
Place the diagonal vanishing point *DVP* half way between the vanishing points.
Construct horizontal square *YNZX* with lines drawn from the vanishing points to intersect on a line from *DVP*. Raise verticals at corners.
Rotate the diagonal of the square upward 45° to *z* and draw a horizontal. This gives us the diagonal plane *YZBA* of the cube.
Draw perspective lines to complete cube.

The 30-60° view
Bisect the distance between the vanishing points to locate one measuring point *MP-Y;* bisect the distance from *MP-Y* to locate the perpendicular *X;* and bisect the distance from *X* to locate second measuring point *MP-Z.*
Draw perspective lines to construct the nearest angle *N* on *X.*
Lay off the height of the cube *NA* and rotate it to a measuring line drawn through *N,* locating *y* and *z.*
Draw lines from *y* to *MP-Y* and *z* to *MP-Z,* locating the side angles *Y* and *Z.*
Complete the cube.

The parallel view
Bisect the distance between the vanishing points to locate diagonal vanishing point *DVP.*
Draw the front edge of the cube *YZ* parallel to the horizon and rotate it up 90° to *z* to find the height of the cube.
Draw perspective lines from *VP-R* to *Y* and *Z.*
Find the diagonal *XZ* of the cube by drawing a perspective line from *DVP.*
Complete the cube.

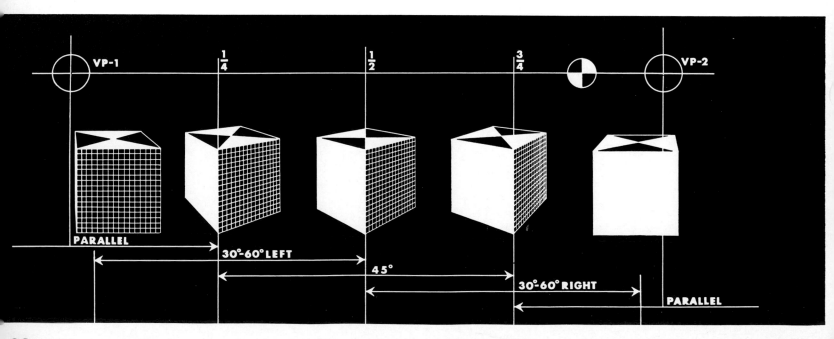

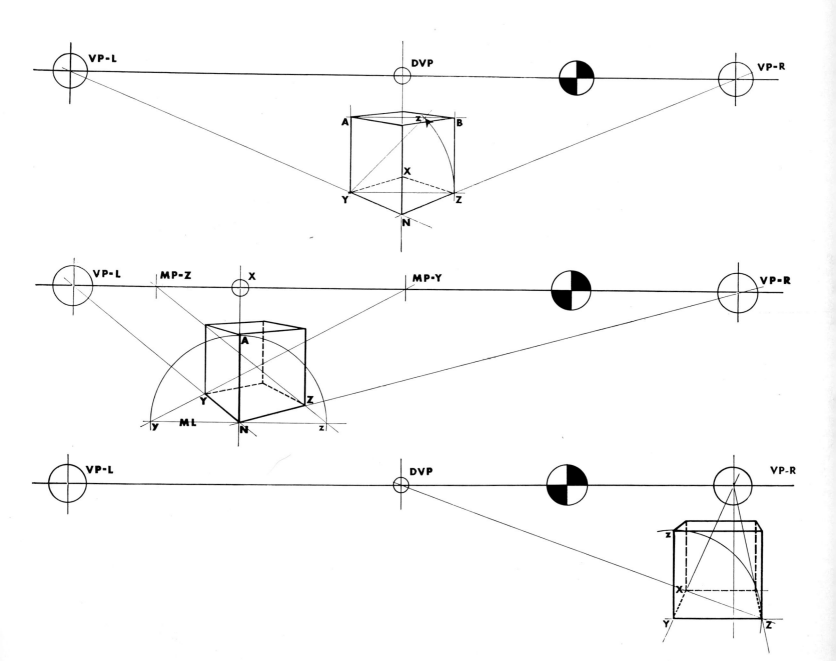

Any object can be rotated 90° between one set of
vanishing points by using the parallel,
30-60°, 45° 30-60°, and parallel cases in order.
In choosing the one view that will show an object
to best advantage we can be guided by
several considerations, 45° perspective serves well
if the object is wider than it is deep; it gives a
good view of both sides without being
monotonous. 30-60° perspective helps avoid
monotony if depth and width are almost equal, and
is useful where one side contains most of the
interest. Parallel perspective is used mainly for
interiors and street scenes, but may be used for
objects if they are very long and must fit a
narrow frame.

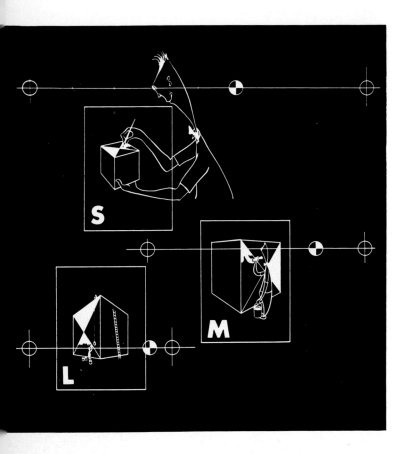

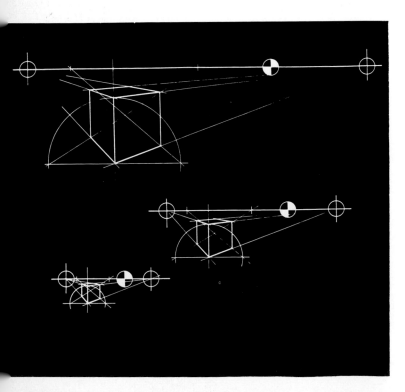

Scale

One advantage of perspective drawings is the impression they give of the scale of objects. The draftsman should know how to control his drawing so that this impression is an accurate one. Scale, in perspective, is a factor of eye level and convergence. It can be assumed that all objects fall into three categories—small (clocks, jewelry, etc.), medium (automobiles, furniture, etc.), and large (buildings, ships, bridges). Convergence will be slight in small objects because they intercept so little of our cone of vision. It will be greater in medium-sized objects and considerable in large objects. Since the eye level of the observer is normally about five feet, it will usually be well above small objects, near the top of medium-sized objects, and near the base of large objects.

Thus a small object will ordinarily have the horizon high on the board and the vanishing points far apart in relation to the drawing. For medium-scale objects, the vanishing points will be closer together, and since they usually straddle the horizon, it will be slightly above the center of the drawing. Large objects are most impressive with eye level near the base of the drawing and the vanishing points close together to give a good deal of convergence. Sometimes, of course, the scale is intentionally upset to achieve dramatic effects.

Size

The size of the drawing depends directly on the distance between the vanishing points. Since the distance between the vanishing points is also a function of scale, a large drawing of a small object means a very large distance between the vanishing points. With a little practice, the draftsman will be able to judge how far the vanishing points should be spread and how high the horizon should be to achieve the proper scale and size for any object. If he is skilled at freehand drawing he may lay out the cube by eye and derive the vanishing points from this sketch before proceeding with the mechanical drawing. Drawings can be enlarged by spreading the vanishing points, or by photostating a finished perspective if this is inconvenient.

In setting up a drawing, it is best to decide the view first and set up the cube in proper scale, then check to see if it is the proper size. If the cube is deficient in view, scale, or size it should be corrected at the outset. It is easier to redraw a faulty cube than to salvage a finished drawing.

After the basic perspective cube has been
drawn it can be used as a measuring device to
obtain a figure of any depth, width, and height.
This is accomplished by multiplying and dividing
the original cube.

Multiplication of the cube

1. Extend the sides in the direction of the
new cube or cubes.
2. Choose any square *ACDB* of the original cube
that is in line with the proposed cube and bisect
the common side *DB* by drawing the diagonals
of the square to locate its perspective center *X*
and drawing a perspective line through *X*
to the common side, locating *M*.
3. From an opposite corner *C* of the square
draw a line through *M* to the extended side.
The intersection with the extended side at *B2*
is the depth of the next cube.
4. Complete the new cube with the necessary
perspective lines and verticals.

Division of the cube

1. Find the perspective midpoint of any square
of the cube by drawing the diagonals.
2. Draw perspective lines through the perspective center to divide the square into four equal
squares.
3. Repeat as often as necessary
to complete the division.
If very small divisions are required, the following
is a quicker method:
1. Mark off the divisions on a vertical of the
cube and draw perspective lines through them.
2. Draw two diagonals of the cube to intersect
the perspective lines and draw verticals through
the intersections.

Multiplication and division may be repeated as
often as desired to create any combination of
dimensions. In every case, the artist must determine which method is best from the proportions of the object he is drawing. Multiplication
would be best if the object were 10 x 1 x 1, for
example, while division would be quickest if it
were 10 x 10 x 1. If the object is almost a cube,
it is easier to draw the largest mass first and
divide to find whatever irregularities may
occur. In general, division is safer and may
prevent exceeding the limits of accurate
drawing.

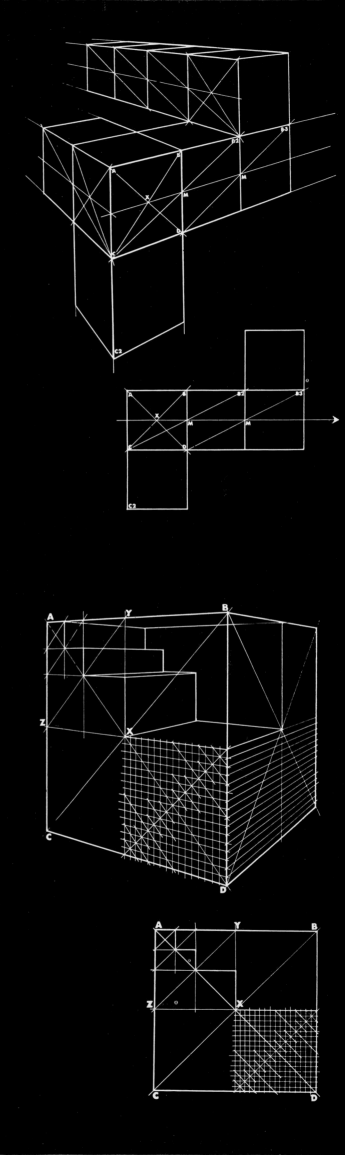

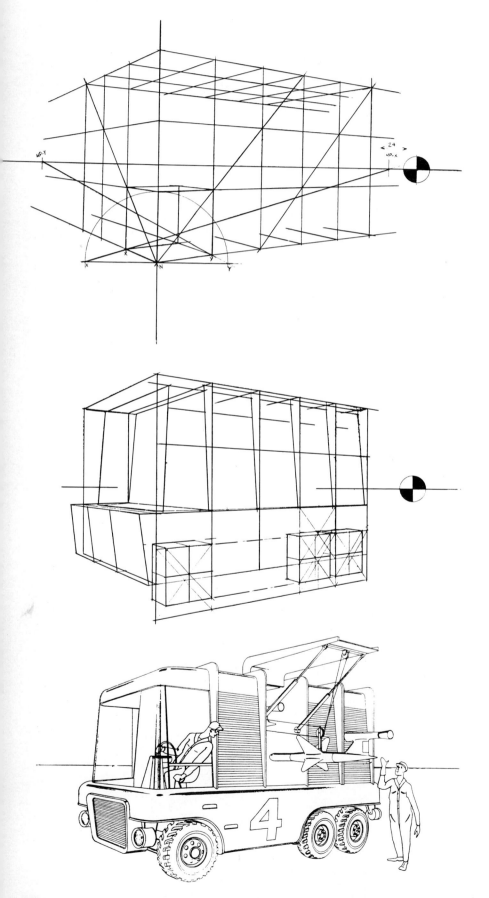

Example 1: a large object

The design of a truck has been settled to some extent in a rough. We want to convert this into a tight and accurate perspective drawing. First, we must choose our view. We want to show something of the front of the truck but are most interested in the side, and a 30-60° view seems the logical choice. Next, we consider the scale of the truck. Our drawing is intended to describe it accurately rather than dramatize its size. Presuming that the truck is about 12 feet high, we decide to place its midpoint slightly above eye level. It will fill as much of the cone of vision as possible. Finally, we decide on the best size for the finished drawing. We do not want the drawing to be cumbersome, but it must be of workable size for the amount of detail that will be included. In this case, we plan a drawing of medium size, about 18 inches across. Having made these preliminary decisions, we start by drawing a horizon fairly low on the table and placing two vanishing points on it 24 inches apart. Now we draw our basic 30-60° cube. The basic cube should be the largest unit that can be multiplied conveniently. We must watch out particularly for three errors: the final form must not cross the midpoint between the vanishing points; it must not come too close to the left-hand vanishing point; and the nearest angles at top and bottom must not approach 90°. We know that the ratio of the truck's width to its length is 3:5; therefore the largest convenient cube will be a third of the width and a fifth of the length. This cube is multiplied to form a grid the over-all size of the truck, and details are added by further multiplication and division. (Rounded forms will be discussed in the next chapter.)

Example 2: a small object

We start with two orthographic views of a
pencil sharpener. Although the subject is
smaller than the previous one and requires less
detail, the drawing is for presentation and
we wish it to be approximately the same size.
In order to achieve the proper sense of
scale, we must place the object well below
eye level and spread the vanishing points far
apart. To begin with, we set up a horizon
near the top of the board and place the
vanishing points about 48 inches apart. We
decide on a 45° view because it will show
both sides well, yet will not be monotonous
since the object is about twice as long as it
is wide. A cube equal to the desired width
of the sharpener is constructed from the
horizon, and from it a figure of the proper
proportions is developed.

This demonstration, like the one opposite, could
be carried much further. In order to show the
mechanisms inside the upper half, for instance,
the original perspective grid could be broken
down to extremely fine dimensions.

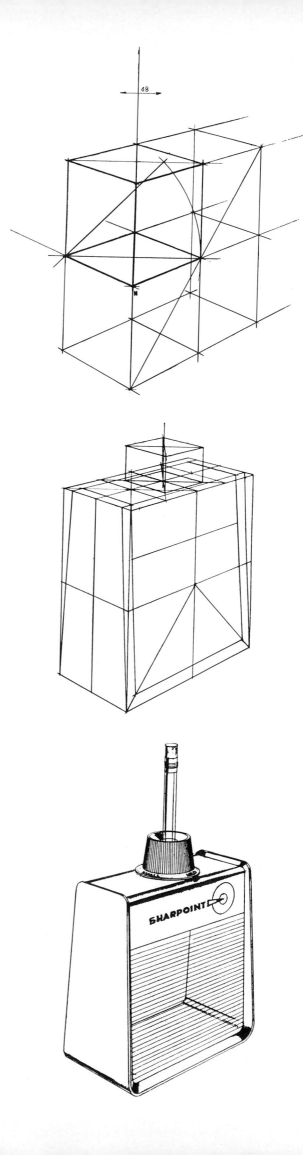

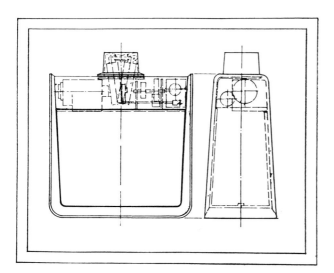

Neither of these drawings was based on a
predetermined scale situation: that is, a
given size of drawing, a given scale of observer,
or a given distance from eye level. This is
easily accomplished, however, and is
explained at the back of the book.

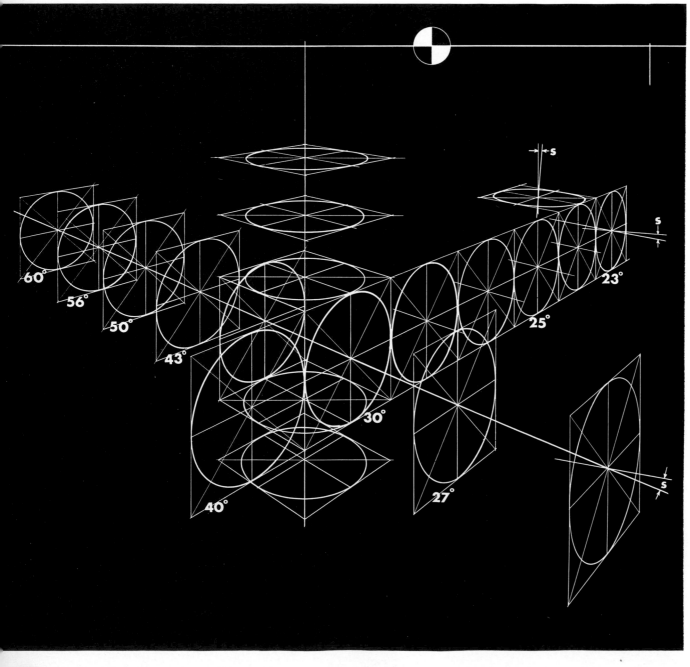

Circular forms

Any object, regardless of its shape, can be broken down into combinations of circular and rectangular forms. We have already learned how to draw rectangular forms. To understand circular forms, examine a circle drawn in a square in elevation. We notice two things:
1. The center of the circle coincides with the intersection of the diagonals of the square (O).
2. The circle is tangent at the midpoint of the four sides of the square $(w, x, y, \text{and } z)$.
The square is the only rectilinear figure which will fulfill these two conditions. To draw a perspective circle, we need only transpose these conditions to a perspective square.

Construction of a circle in perspective

1. Draw any perspective square ABCD.
2. Draw diagonals to locate the center.
3. Draw perspective lines through the perspective center to bisect the sides $(w, x, y, \text{and } z)$.
4. Draw a smooth curve tangent to the midpoints of the sides. This curve will be a circle in perspective.

The ellipse

Ordinarily, we would use a French curve to draw a smooth curve. However, it can be shown that any curve inscribed in a perspective square as described above is an ellipse. If we can find a simple way of matching an ellipse to a perspective square, we can use an ellipse guide for drawing perspective circles. The ellipse has two dimensions that may be useful, a major axis and a minor axis.
Draw ellipses on opposite faces of a perspective cube and connect the perspective centers of these faces with a perspective line. This line, which is perpendicular to both ellipses, crosses them at their narrowest dimensions and is thus the minor axis of both.
Now draw two concentric circles in perspective and locate their major and minor axes. Notice that while the minor axes are on the same line, the major axes $(m \text{ and } M)$ are erratic.
According to these two figures, the major axis of the ellipse is of no value in perspective drawing. The minor axis, on the other hand, is easily located: we need only find the perspective center of the square and draw a perspective perpendicular at this point.
Parallel circles have minor axes on a line.
To use the ellipse guide in drawing a perspective circle, choose the ellipse that is tangent at the midpoint of all four sides of the perspective square, and whose minor axis coincides with the perspective perpendicular.

The drawing opposite illustrates two reasons why the ellipse guide may not fulfill both these conditions at the same time:
1. An accurate ellipse will not fit a distorted square. In previous chapters we have seen how distortion increases as the cube is shifted from side to side.
2. Ellipse guides usually come in increments of 5°; the required ellipse may fall somewhere in between.

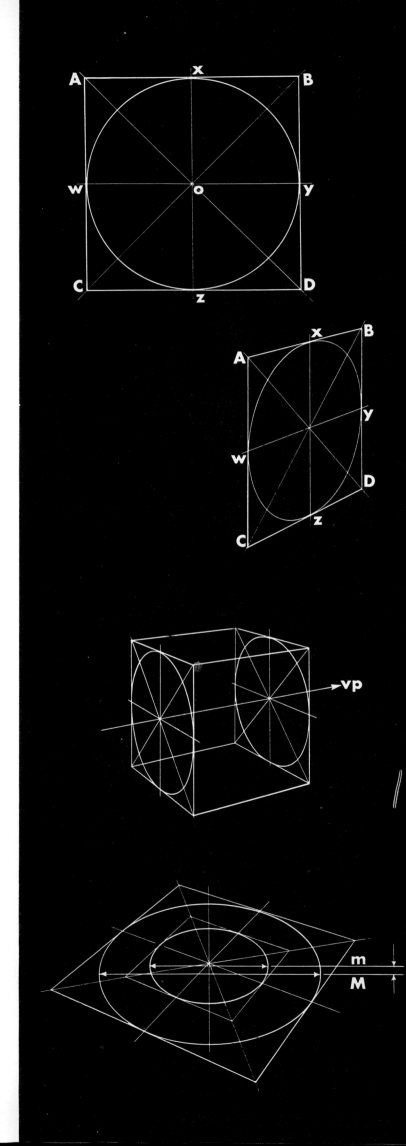

CIRC   Choice of methods for drawing perspective circles

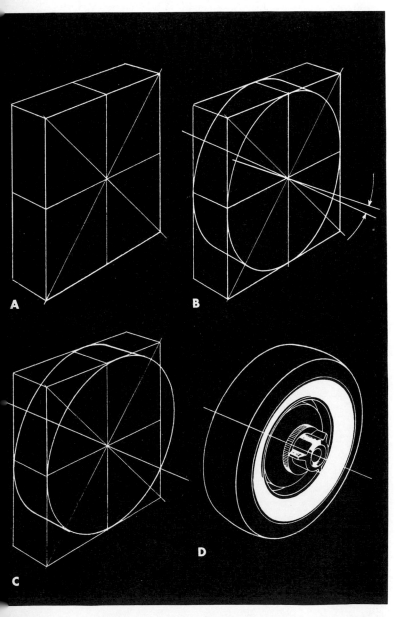

We have seen that a perspective circle is an ellipse inscribed in a perspective square so that it is tangent at the midpoint of the sides of the square and its minor axis is the perspective perpendicular of the square.

If we find that the ellipse guide does not provide an ellipse that fulfills these two conditions, we have two choices: We can use the ellipse that comes closest to fitting the square when its minor axis is properly lined up, or we can draw a smooth curve tangent to the midpoints of the sides of the square, overlooking the probable error in minor axis. Generally speaking, the tangent-drawn curve will look better than the true ellipse, but it may be unwieldly to produce, and the draftsman must decide in each case what is the best method for drawing an acceptable perspective circle.

Suppose, for example, that we are drawing an automobile wheel. If the front wheel is in true perspective, it is not unusual for the rear wheel to be slightly in error. This wheel may involve as many as fifteen concentric ellipses, and it obviously will save time if we can use the ellipse guides. After we have drawn the original perspective square (A), we can see how much error there is by drawing a tangent curve ellipse (B) and comparing its minor axis with the perspective perpendicular.

In practice we would disregard the small error and use the ellipse guides. We choose the ellipse that fits best when the minor axis is properly aligned (C) and finally complete the wheel by lining up a series of concentric ellipses along the same minor axis (D).

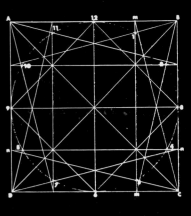

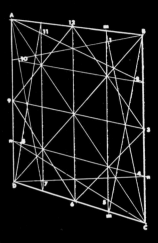

The twelve-point ellipse

Occasionally it is necessary to draw an ellipse
larger than those found on ellipse guides. As an
aid to drawing a smooth curve in such cases
the draftsman can locate eight additional points
on the ellipse by geometric construction. To see
how this is done, let us start with a circle in
a square:

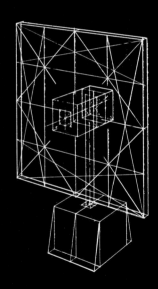

1. Draw a square *ABCD* and draw the
diagonals to locate its center. Draw a circle
tangent to the sides of the square.
2. Divide the square into quadrants by
connecting the midpoints of the sides.
3. Locate the center of each quadrant by
drawing the diagonals.
4. Draw horizontals and verticals through the
center of each quadrant (*mm* and *nn,*
for example).
5. Draw line *Cm. Its intersection* with *nn* will
lie on the circle. Similarly, the intersection of
Cn with *mm* will lie on the circle. By repeating
this construction, eight points on the circle
can be located in addition to the original
tangent points.
When this construction is carried out with a
perspective square, it locates eight points on
the ellipse inscribed in that square.

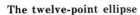

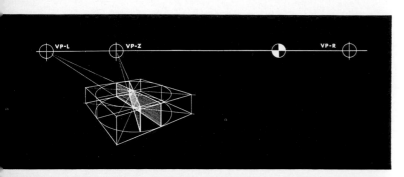

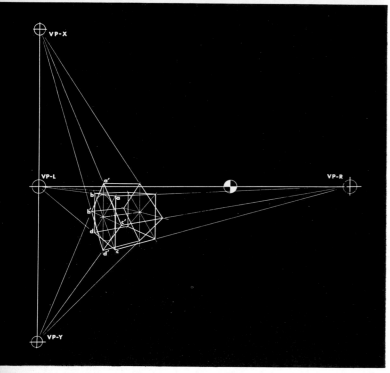

Rotation

The ellipse is used to rotate planes or solid figures which are turned in relation to the basic perspective, such as pullman chairs, steering wheels, house roofs, box lids, etc. When an object is rotated on the horizontal plane the vanishing point or points are shifted along the horizon. To illustrate horizontal rotation, we will rotate a plane:

1. Construct a perspective square around the center of rotation of the plane and inscribe an ellipse in it. Construct additional ellipses intersecting all important points on the plane.
2. On the initial ellipse, plot the amount of rotation desired by construction or by judgment. From this point on the ellipse draw a line through the center of rotation to the horizon, locating the new vanishing point *VP-Z*.
4. Complete the new figure using the new vanishing point.

Rotation in a vertical plane is more complex because it usually throws the object into three-point perspective. The new vanishing points are directly above or below one of the original vanishing points. To illustrate vertical rotation, we will rotate a cube 45°.

1. Draw a vertical through *VP-L*.
2. Inscribe an ellipse on side *abcd* of the cube.
3. Where the ellipse crosses diagonal *ad* of the side, draw a tangent *b'd'* and extend it until it intersects the vertical, locating *VP-X*. *VP-X* is the vanishing point of *b'd'* and its parallels.
4. Where the ellipse crosses diagonal *cb* draw a tangent to locate *VP-Y*.
5. Complete the cube, using vanishing points *VP-X*, *VP-Y*, and *VP-R*.

Four forms

The four basic forms of which all objects are composed are the cube, the cylinder, the cone, and the sphere. By applying ellipses to the basic rectilinear form, we generate the remaining three forms.

The cylinder and the cone require that a circle be drawn on one or both ends of a rectilinear figure. The sphere is unique because in any perspective it remains a circle in outline.

The ellipses are its equators; its outline is drawn from the perspective center of the cube and is tangent to the extremities of the ellipses.

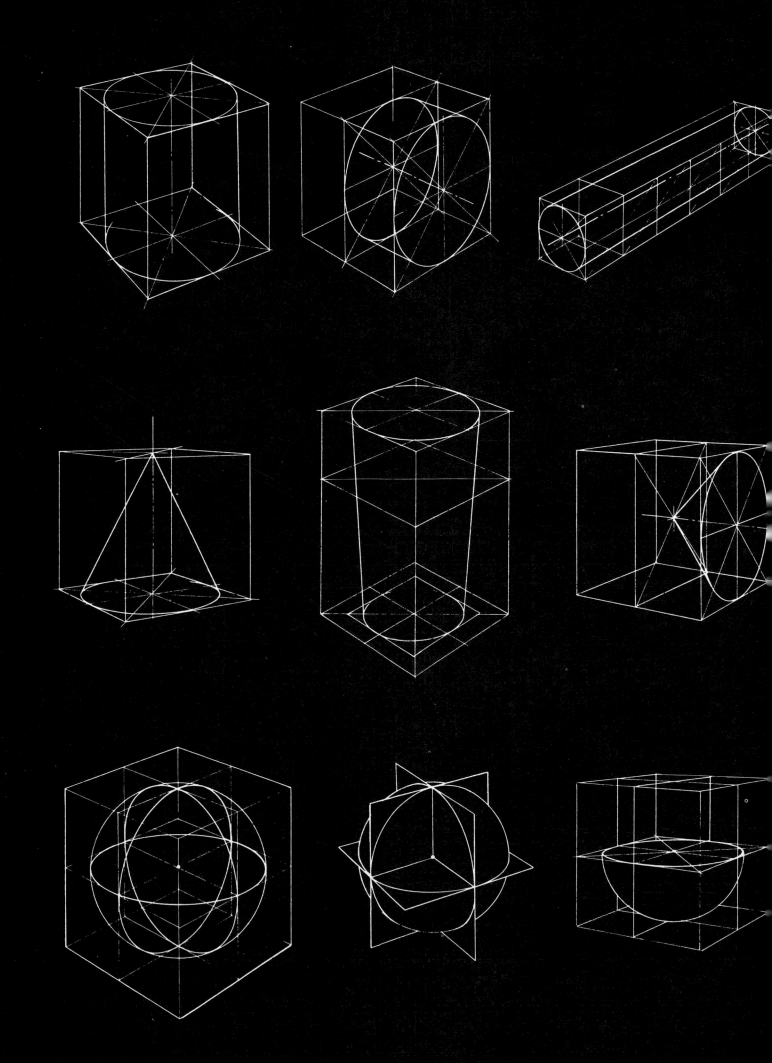

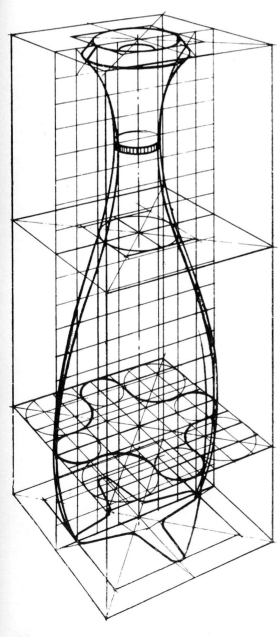

The best way to draw compound forms like those shown here is to develop a perspective grid on which the curves can be plotted from one or more scale drawings. The example at right is a fairly simple one because the cross section is circular and does not need to be derived from a scale drawing. We start with a longitudinal section showing the free curving side in true scale and translate this curve to a perspective grid. Details are developed by multiplication and division in subsequent tracings. Finally, the circular cross-section is derived by constructing a series of ellipses tangent to the free curve with their centers on the main axis of the figure. The final outline is at the extremities of these ellipses.

An object composed of free curves in more than one plane, like that at left, requires a complex grid in three dimensions. In this case the final outline was traced on a grid made by superimposing four horizontal sections on a vertical section. Usually only a few curves need be plotted accurately and the rest can be filled in by eye.

When he is designing directly in perspective, the designer can plot some basic curves on a perspective grid and try out variations on an overlay sheet. The system is invaluable where curved forms must envelope a given mechanism — in an electric shaver, for instance. In such cases, grids are drawn at critical points to make sure the curved form clears the mechanism.

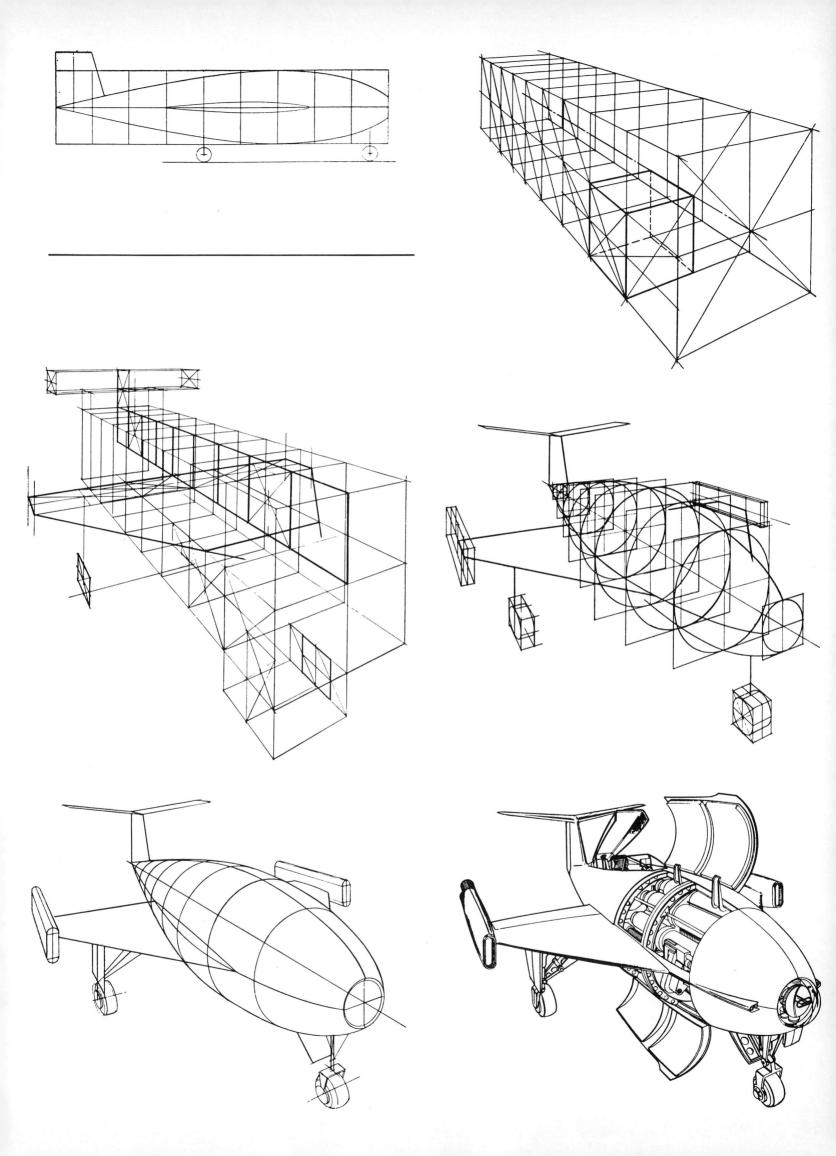

Introduction to three-point perspective

Three-point perspective

In ordinary two-point perspective, only two vanishing points are required. Some of the lines in the cube converge toward one of these vanishing points, some toward the other. A third set of lines — usually the vertical ones — do not converge at all but are parallel to each other. Their vanishing point is assumed to be at an infinite distance from the observer. In three-point perspective, a finite vanishing point is provided for all three sets of lines in the cube.

Three-point perspective should be used a good deal more than it is. Parallel lines appear parallel in perspective only if they happen also to be parallel to the picture plane, and in most positions the cube has no edges parallel to the picture plane. In other words, two-point perspective can be regarded as a special case of three-point perspective. It is used more than three-point perspective mainly because the latter is so much more difficult.

To understand three-point perspective examine this case: We want to draw a group of cubes suspended at various points between eye level and the plan view. Since the observer is looking squarely at the top cube, its verticals are perpendicular to his line of sight and parallel to the picture plane, and they appear parallel in perspective. If these verticals are parallel all the others must be; thus all four cubes are in two-point perspective. If the four cubes are lined up with their nearest edges against the picture plane, all the nearest edges are the same height, regardless of their relation to the observer.

Now suppose we are drawing four separate pictures of these four cubes. In this case the observer doesn't have to maintain a fixed position, and he naturally turns toward each cube as he draws it. Since by definition the picture plane is perpendicular to the observer's line of sight, it rotates to a new position for each cube. The top cube is still in two-point perspective, but the second and third cubes are at random angles to the picture plane; they are in three-point perspective.

The second drawing shows that a cube whose sides are perfectly vertical is in two-point perspective when it is straddling the horizon. If it is below the horizon (as most small objects are) it is seen at an angle and there is convergence in every pair of lines. Returning to the first drawing, we can easily see how the two-point cube grows more and more distorted as it drops away from the observer's line of sight.

The draftsman often permits considerable distortion rather than introduce the third vanishing point because three-point perspective is complicated and space-consuming. In addition to a large horizontal area it usually requires tremendous depth for a third vanishing point.

The drawings at the left compare two-point and three-point drawings of one object seen from one angle. Although the second drawing is more dramatic, the convergence is slight in an object so close to eye level, and we do not object to the distortion in the first drawing. Vertical convergence is more important in objects that are taller than they are wide. It is imperative in objects so far below eye level that more of the top is seen than the sides.

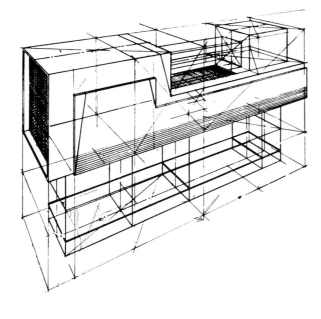

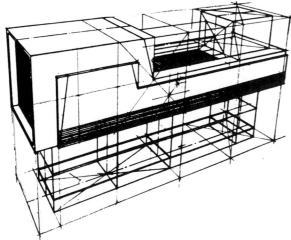

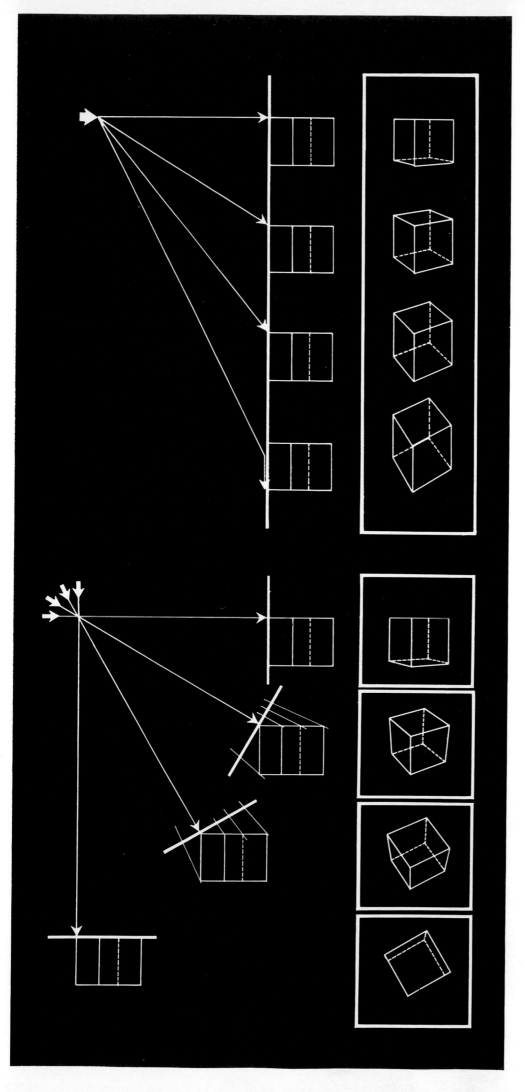

Construction of the cube in three-point perspective

A cube in three-point perspective is derived from three horizons. These horizons are the three sides of an acute triangle. The vertices of the triangle are vanishing points. Its altitudes are measuring lines perpendicular to each horizon, and their intersection marks the nearest angle of the cube.

Construction of the cube in three-point perspective

1. Draw a horizon and place two vanishing points *VP-L* and *VP-R* on it.
2. Bisect the distance between *VP-L* and *VP-R* and from midpoint *m* draw a circle through them.
3. At any point *X* between the vanishing points, depending on the view desired, draw a vertical measuring line; its intersection with the circle locates the station point *SP-X*.
4. Draw lines from *VP-L* and *VP-R* to intersect on the vertical measuring line, locating nearest angle *n* at the desired distance below eye level. Continue these lines to the circle, finding points *Y* and *Z*.
5. From *VP-L* draw a line through *Z* to the vertical measuring line. Repeat for *VP-R* and *Y*. The two lines will meet on the vertical measuring line at the third vanishing point *VP-3*. We now have three horizons, each with its vanishing points and its measuring line (at *X*, *Y*, and *Z*). We found the station point for one horizon on a circle drawn through the vanishing points. To find the other two station points we draw similar circles.
6. Bisect the horizon between *VP-R* and *VP-3* and draw a circle through them. Station point *SP-Y* will be found where this circle intersects the measuring line through *Y*.
7. Repeat for the horizon between *VP-L* and *VP-3*, locating station point *SP-Z*.
8. Connect all the vanishing points with their station points, enclosing a cube.
9. Although this cube is accurate, it cannot be used because the corners at *SP-X*, *SP-Y*, and *SP-Z* are 90° angles and therefore at the limits of true perspective. To make usable cubes or a grid, we must subdivide it.

This method is accurate for any view of the cube, but it is cumbersome. Usually the draftsman can save time by using one of several special cases and short cuts.

The perfect 45° view

In one case of three-point perspective the cube is perfectly symmetrical. This happens when it is rotated at 45° with respect to each of the three horizons. Then front corner and rear corner coincide on the observer's line of sight; lines converge toward each vanishing point at equal angles; and corresponding corners are at equal distances from the eye. Construction of this cube is quick and accurate.

1. Draw a circle and place the nearest angle *n* of the cube at its center.
2. From *n* draw three measuring lines at 120°, locating the three vanishing points, and co-incidentally the three station points, on the circle. The front edges of the cube will lie on these lines.
3. Connect perspective lines at any point *X* on one of the measuring lines. Draw perspective lines to meet at the same angle on the other measuring lines, and the cube is completed.

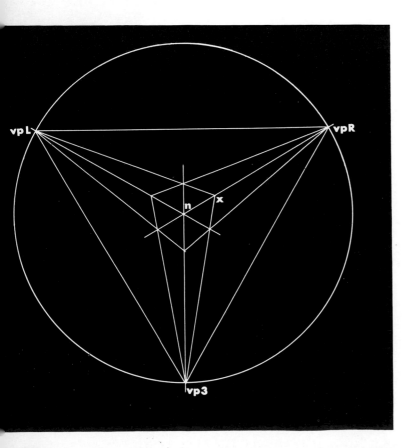

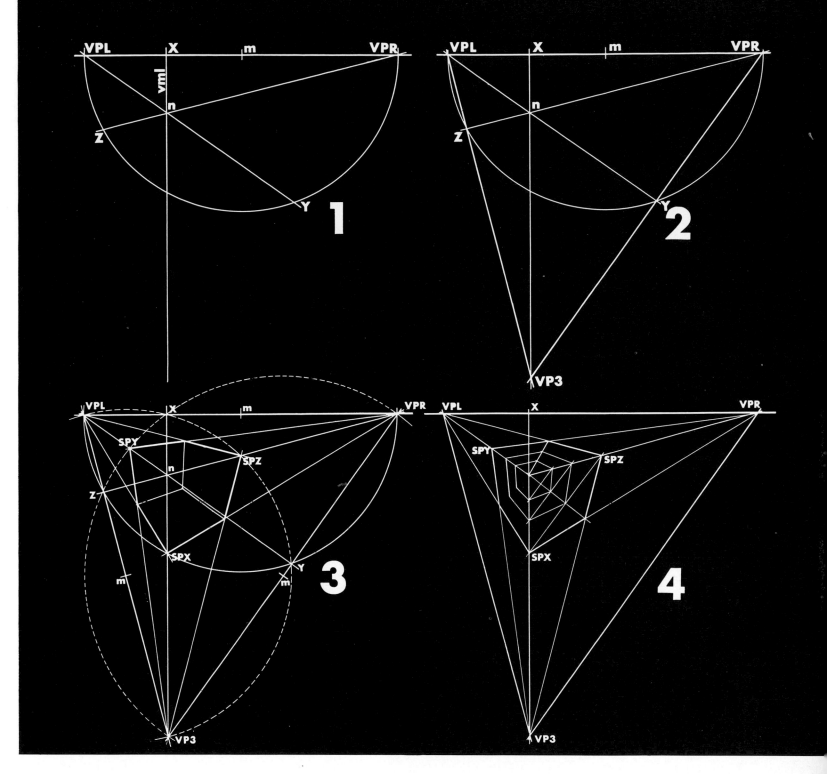

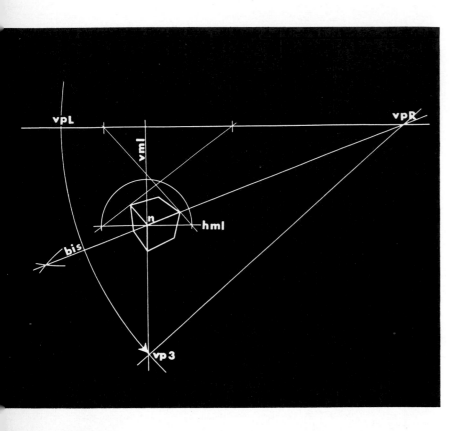

The combination 45° and 30-60° view

A second special case of three-point perspective is the combination of a 45° view toward one horizon and a 30-60° view toward another. This view is less monotonous than the straight 45° view, but somewhat more complicated to draw.

1. Draw a horizon and divide it according to the usual 30-60° method to find the vanishing points, the measuring points, and the vertical measuring line.
2. Rotate the distance between the vanishing points to the vertical measuring line to find VP-3.
3. Draw the bisector of this arc. Its intersection with the vertical measuring line places the nearest angle n.
4. Draw a horizontal measuring line through n and complete the 30-60° horizontal square as usual.
5. Complete another side of the cube by drawing lines from VPL and VP-3 to meet on the bisector. The bisector is the diagonal of this side, and since it is half way between two vanishing points, the side is in 45° perspective.
6. Complete the cube.

Three-point perspective by trained eye

The two short-cuts just given are a help in producing two specific views of the cube in three-point perspective. A third short-cut can be used to draw the cube in a variety of positions. Basically, it is a method for introducing vertical convergence into a cube drawn in two-point perspective. It is not a mathematically accurate method, but depends partly on skillful judgment.

1. Draw a cube A-B in two-point perspective at any angle close to eye level.
2. Draw diagonals to find its midpoint M.
3. Rotate one vertical edge inward until it looks right for the distance below eye level.
4. Where the new edge intersects its diagonal (C) draw a new bottom plane for the cube, using the original vanishing points. Draw all the sides in to it.

This system assures that the vanishing point is directly under the cube, and that the foreshortening of the vertical distance is at least roughly in proportion to the convergence. It is most useful for objects near eye level, where vertical convergence might not be worth the trouble of a more elaborate method. In objects well below eye level, where vertical convergence is essential, the skilled eye is not adequate, and the orthodox method must be followed.

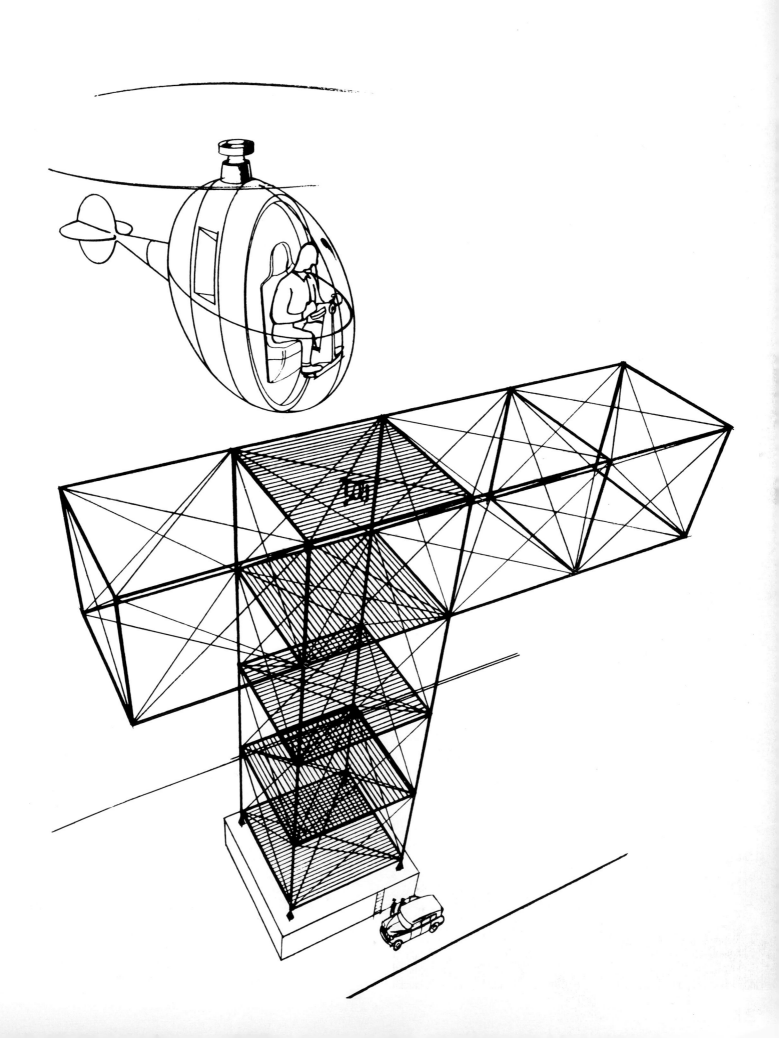

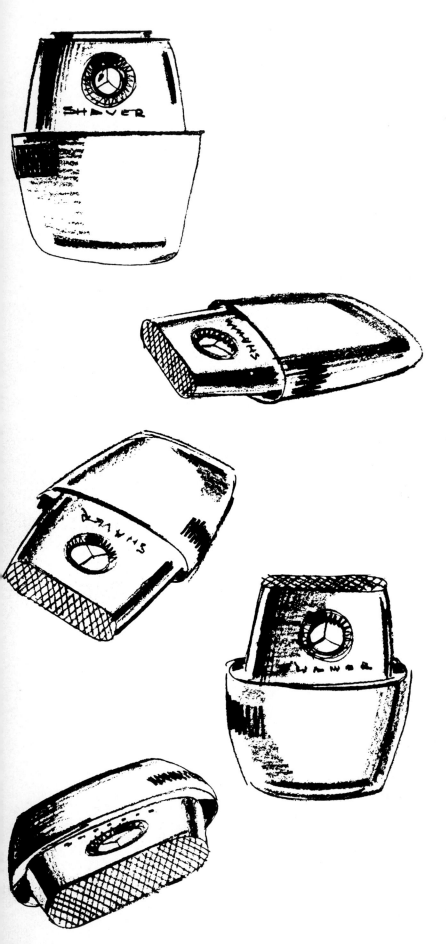

Visualization

No matter how thoroughly he knows mechanical perspective, the draftsman must always rely on his own eye. Usually his first step in making a drawing is to sketch the object at various angles to help in deciding the best view. Often the "best" view is a matter of opinion, and if someone else has to okay the drawing it is a good idea to know his choice before the final drawing is begun.

At left is a typical series of preliminary sketches for an electric shaver. Each has its advantages, and any one of them might be chosen. The first would be the simplest to make because it is actually a mechanical plan view, and although it does not show the cross section, it gives the most accurate view of the face. The second shows the three most interesting sides with equal emphasis. The third shows the same three sides but emphasizes the face. The fourth is essentially a plan view, like the first, with a bare indication of the cross-section added. The final view is the least informative but the most dramatic—a shaver's eye view.

If he wants the most generally informative view the artist will probably choose the third. It is not an especially dramatic view to start with, but when the drawing is completed, the artist can turn it to find a more effective view. On the opposite page, it is shown upside down, so that the shaver seems to be floating in air instead of lying on a table. A round mat helps to spotlight it.

The cold eye

When he is constructing a perspective drawing the artist must check constantly to see that it *looks* right. The eye grows tired from looking at a drawing for a long time, but there are various ways of giving it a fresh outlook. One of the best is a diminishing glass, which makes the drawing much smaller, frames it, and gives the work an entirely new appearance, so that bad proportions or a poor choice of view show up immediately. A more complex way of checking the work, but a useful one if the drawing is to be reproduced in a smaller size, is to make photostats, particularly negatives. A simple way of refreshing the eye is to look at the drawing in a mirror, or, if the paper is sufficiently transparent, simply to turn it over. When the artist is drawing at a large board, and particularly when he is seated, he should put the drawing on the wall or stand on his stool from time to time so that he does not always see the drawing in perspective. This is particularly important when he is doing a large three-point perspective, since vertical convergence is especially likely to be distorted if the drawing is always viewed at an angle.

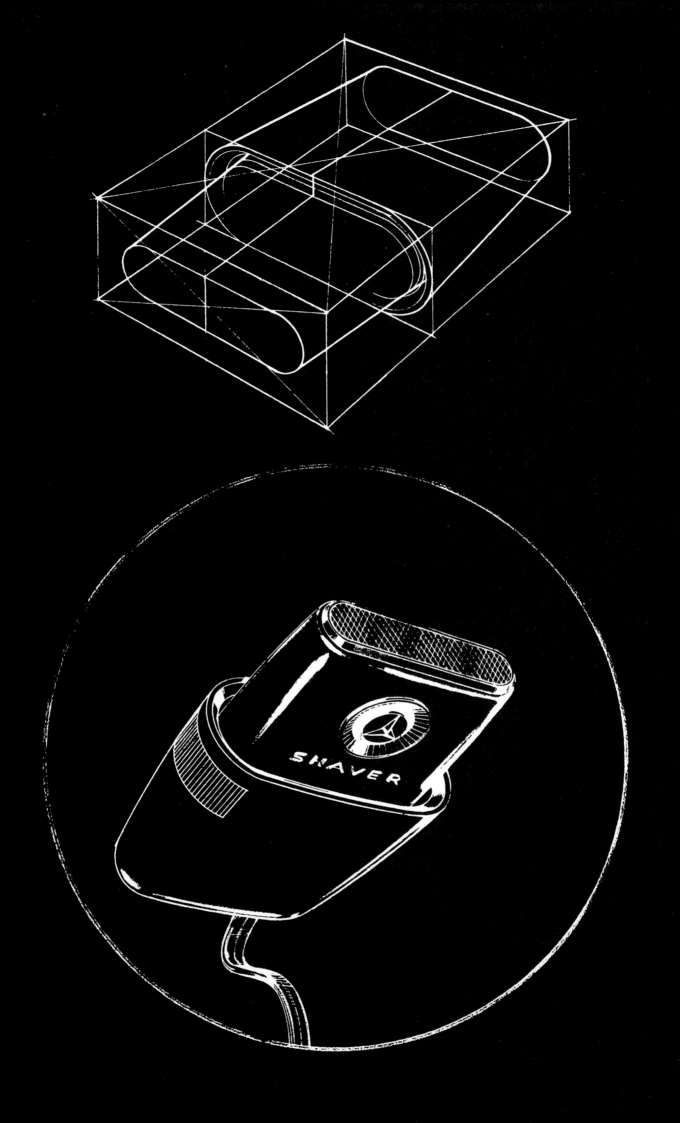

Ordinarily the artist uses his trained eye to make certain that his drawing is accurate; occasionally, his judgment tells him to violate the normal rules of perspective. His ability to do this depends on his complete understanding of these rules and his artistic judgment.

Adding a vanishing point

The drawing at the right illustrates the introduction of a vanishing point in a two-point perspective view. According to the rules we have learned, this means that the drawing extends beyond the limits of accuracy; the vanishing point should only appear in parallel perspective. Yet the vanishing point is bound to appear in a vista as broad as this, and sometimes a certain section of a drawing—a street or a line of buildings—is more effective in parallel perspective. Inevitably, there is distortion in the area around the vanishing point. It is usually not noticeable in flat surfaces like a tile floor or a building facade, but it is painfully apparent in any solid object like the cube at far left in the drawing opposite. It is a good idea to plan the drawing so that there are no solid objects in this area. No matter how carefully he plans, the artist will probably find some eyesores that can only be overcome by trial and error—by his own judgment.

Exaggeration

The use of the vanishing point in two-point perspective is an extreme violation of normal perspective rules. A simpler example is the use of exaggeration for dramatic effect—making objects appear bigger or smaller than they are, or very close or very distant. This is done by manipulating convergence and the distance above or below eye level. If we want to make a truck look particularly imposing, for example, we might draw it very high against the horizon and place the vanishing points close together to exaggerate the convergence. The drawing is not strictly accurate, but it has the desired effect.

FREE   Practice in drawing freehand cubes

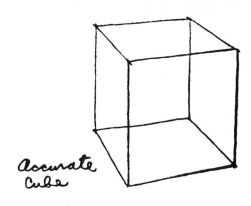

accurate
Cube

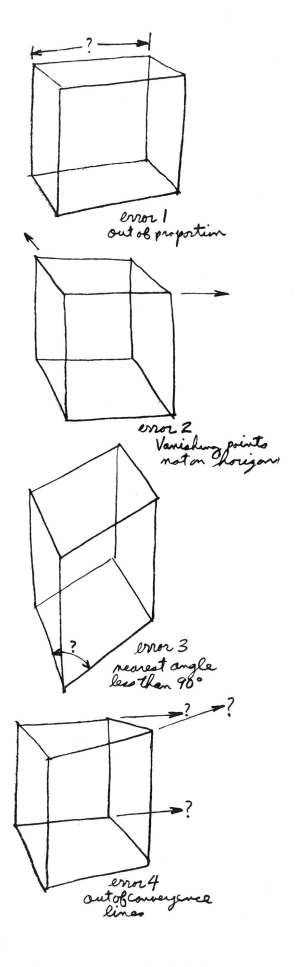

error 1
out of proportion

error 2
Vanishing points
not on horizon

error 3
nearest angle
less than 90°

error 4
out of convergence
lines

Practice in drawing freehand cubes

It is a mistake for anyone to feel he is skilled in perspective until he has mastered freehand drawing. Even mechanical perspective requires a trained eye to check inaccuracies and to judge view, size, and scale. Freehand drawing requires skill in judging all the factors that make up perspective drawing simultaneously. The most important and difficult mental control is the judgment of proportion. The mental processes that control accurate proportion on paper are the same as those that permit the designer to judge good proportion in objects. Thus freehand drawing practice tends to make the designer more sensitive and improve his taste in form, line, curves, etc.

The key to superior freehand drawing is to break through the impulse to copy — either actually or mentally — an outline shape, and to develop a truly three-dimensional concept. The cube is the basic form in freehand work, as in mechanical work. I believe it is best to begin freehand practice without any guides, such as vanishing points or horizons. As a first exercise I ask students to draw dozens of cubes in a variety of positions. These are then divided into four groups according to four basic errors. The student soon learns to recognize these errors immediately and avoid them while he is making the drawing.

1. Proportion. Carefully inspect each side of the cube for squareness. The most oblique sides are the most difficult to judge. It is a help to draw the diagonals of each side. If the nearest angle is at 45° to the observer, the diagonals should be horizontal and vertical; their proper relationship at other rotations can be learned by observing them in mechanical drawings.
2. Tilted horizon. Even though the verticals are truly vertical on the paper, they are not necessarily vertical to the horizon. This error, which is eliminated in mechanical perspective by the use of instruments, can be a subtle and annoying source of trouble in freehand drawing. It is discovered by extending the sides of the cube to find the vanishing points and the horizon.
3. Nearest angle. In freehand drawing, as in mechanical perspective, the nearest angle must always be greater than 90°.
4. Convergence. Notice that the lines do not all converge at the same vanishing points, giving a warped look to one of the planes. Placing a straightedge on doubtful lines will quickly point out any error.

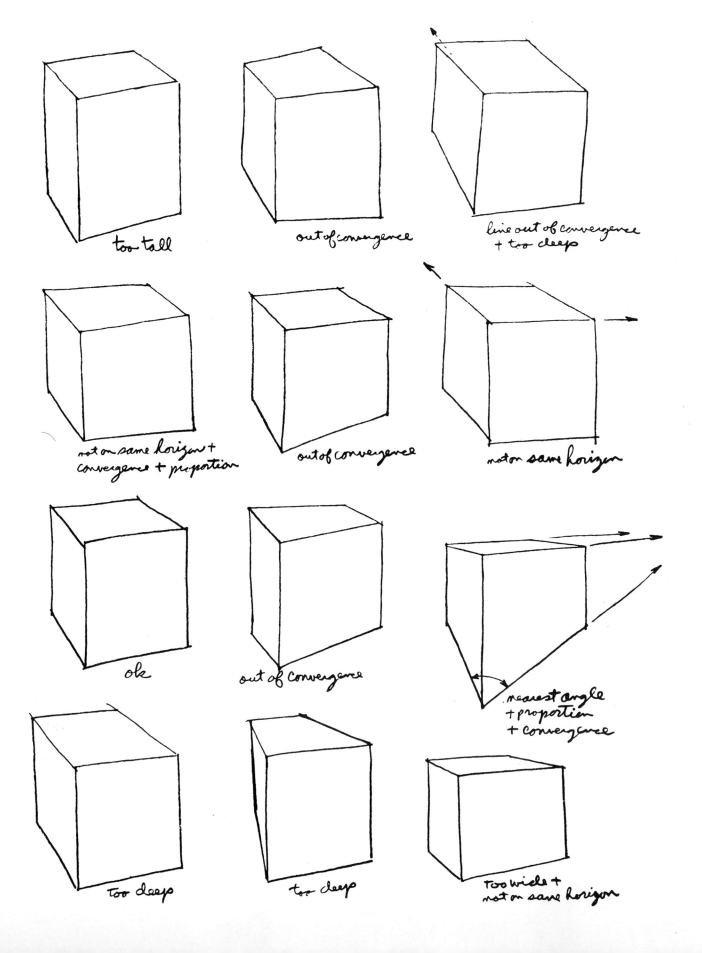

too tall

out of convergence

line out of convergence + too deep

not on same horizon + convergence + proportion

out of convergence

not on same horizon

ok

out of convergence

nearest angle + proportion + convergence

too deep

too deep

too wide + not on same horizon

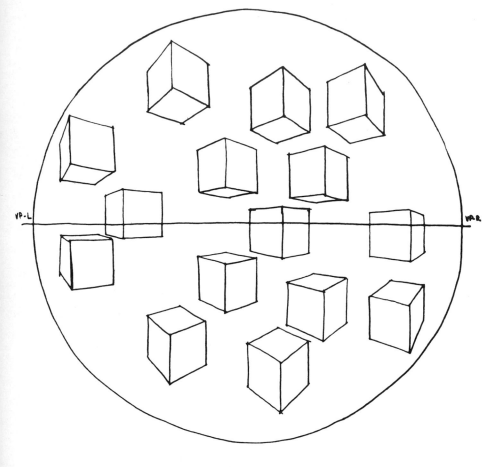

View
Set up two vanishing points and draw many cubes between them. Notice how the relationship of the sides changes as the cubes rotate from one vanishing point to the other. This exercise is also helpful in teaching proportion: since all the other variables are controlled by the position of the vanishing points, the student can concentrate on achieving the proper proportions of the sides.

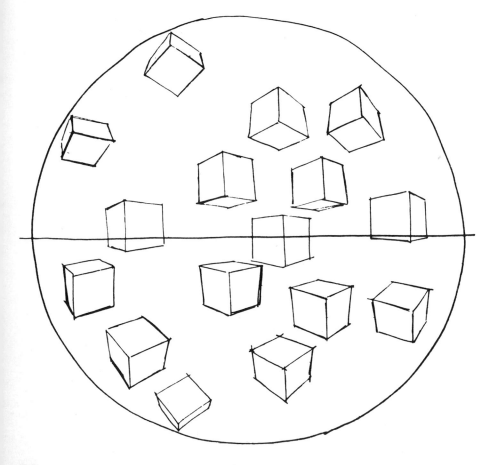

Add a third vanishing point and the parallel view to this exercise.

Scale and size
Draw cubes of approximately the same actual
size to represent small, medium, and large
objects. Notice how the impression of smallness
or bigness depends on convergence and eye
level. Details can be added to enhance
the impression.
The size of the drawing is in direct proportion
to the distance between the vanishing points.
This exercise shows that if objects of varying
size are to be represented in drawings of
similar size the distance between the vanishing
points must vary widely.

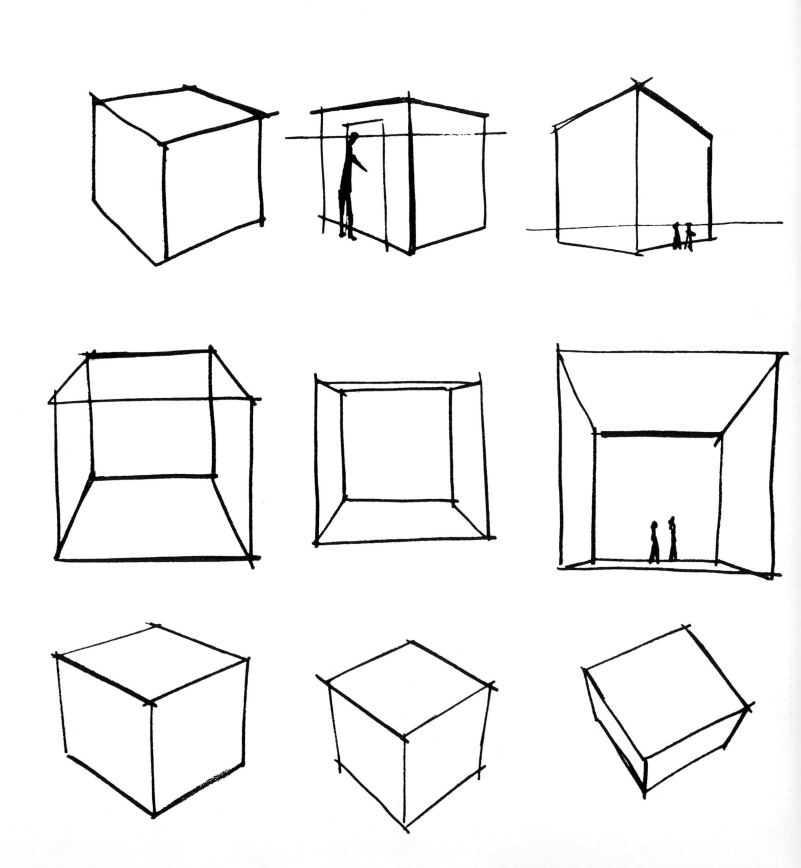

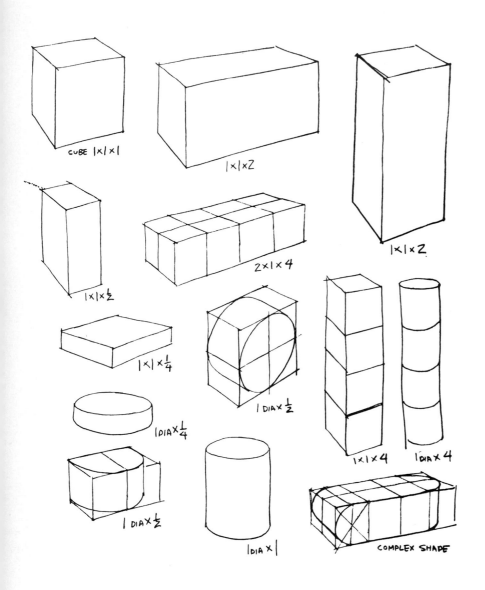

CUBE 1×1×1

1×1×2

1×1×2

1×1×½

2×1×4

1×1×¼

1 DIA×½

1×1×4   1 DIA×4

1 DIA×¼

1 DIA×½

1 DIA×1

COMPLEX SHAPE

Rectilinear forms
When the student can draw the cube with confidence in all positions, he is ready to try more complex rectilinear forms. These should be drawn directly by eye and then broken down by division to a basic cube that can be examined for accuracy. When the draftsman is able to perform this check continually and automatically as he works, he is ready to proceed to the true freehand drawing of any object.

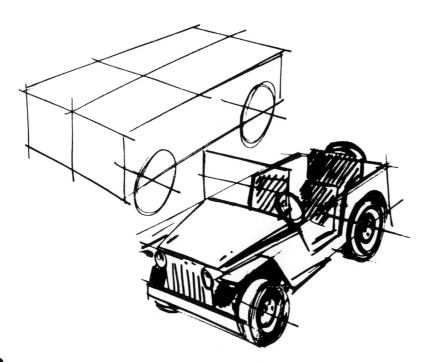

I want to draw a jeep.
Draw a rectilinear form with the proportions of the jeep; then add details in perspective until the drawing is complete.

The ellipse

At the start, draw the ellipse inside a perspective square. After a good deal of practice, forms with circular sections can be drawn directly. The beginner will find that it helps to turn the paper so that the minor axis is vertical and draw the ellipse horizontally against it.

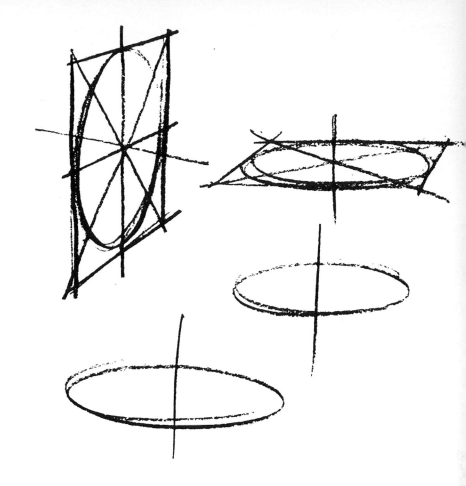

I want to draw a watch

Draw the ellipse directly if advanced enough. Or else draw a rectilinear form of the proper proportions and divide it up with the diagonals and the bisectors of the sides. It takes a real understanding of convergence in the circle to place the numerals properly.

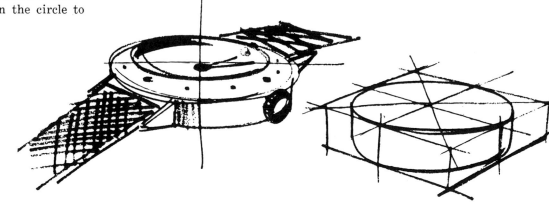

An advanced exercise

As an exercise to climax these skills, practice drawing complex figures upside down. This exercise puts an immense strain on the draftsman's knowledge of freehand drawing.

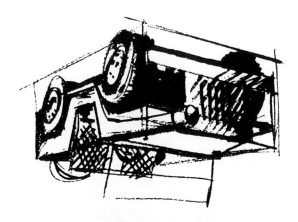

The constant practice that is required to develop and maintain freehand skill can be turned into an amusing pastime. For example, choose an object — as small as a fountain pen or as big as a railway train — and make many drawings of it to see how you can change its appearance by varying view and scale.

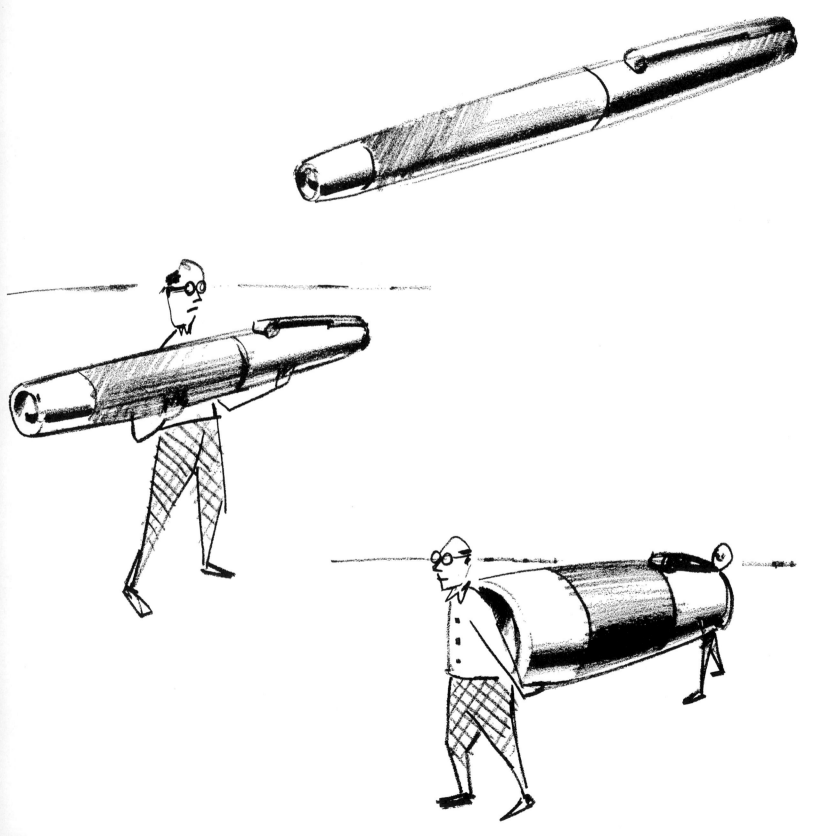

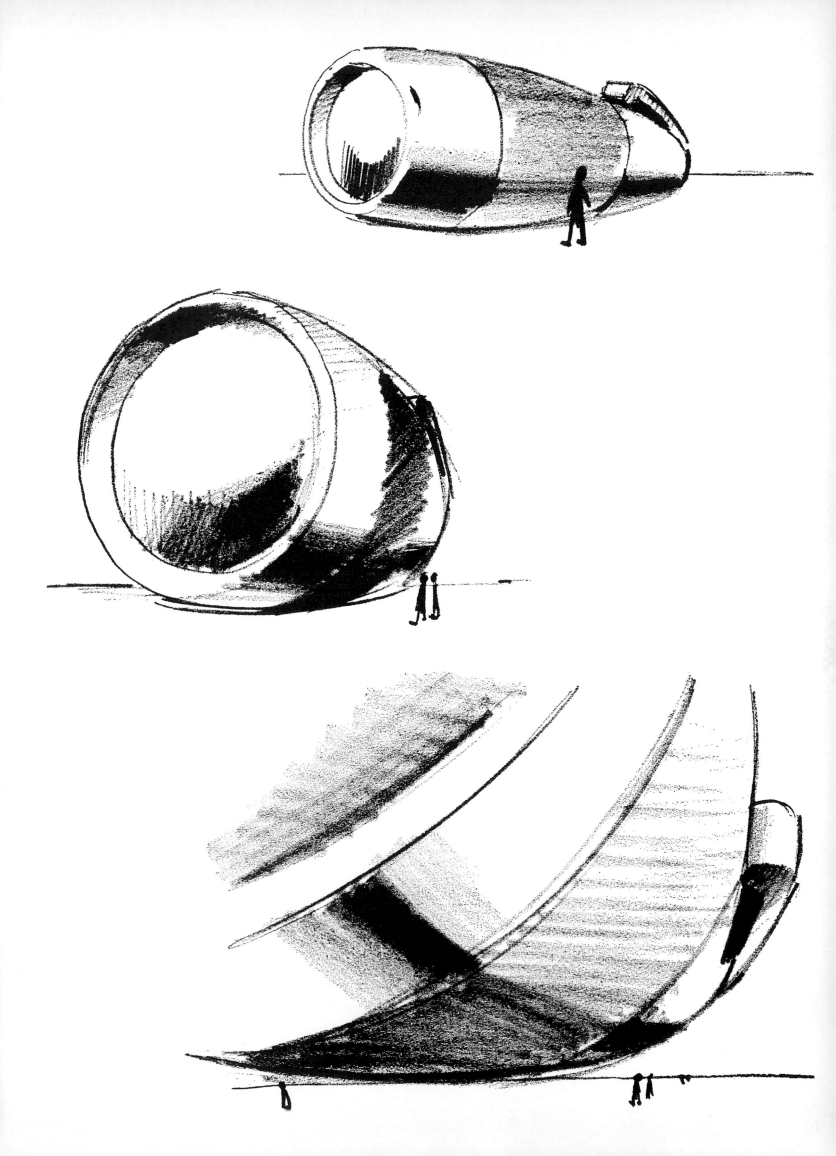

True scale

True scale can be defined as a controlled relationship between three measurements: the distance from the observer to the object, the size of the object, and its distance below or above eye level. Existing systems for achieving true scale are complicated, and usually used only when necessary. But with my perspective system, true scale can easily become an everyday tool in perspective drawing.

Suppose, for example, that we wish to show a console radio in a display room. We can imagine that the machine would be about ten feet away; that it would be about 3′ high and 2′ below eye level. Obviously if we can base our preliminary construction on these measurements we will eliminate trial and error.

To set up the principles of true scale, let us reproduce this situation by the top plan system. First, draw a top plan of a 45° cube at a scale of 3 units to a side. Draw the horizon through the nearest angle, and draw a vertical measuring line perpendicular to the horizon. Measure 10 units down the measuring line to find the station point; measure 2 units down to find the top of the cube and 3 more to find its height. Draw lines from the station point parallel to the sides of the top plan cube to locate the vanishing points, and complete the cube.

Notice that in 45° perspective, the station point and the vanishing points are at equal distances from the top plan cube.

This means that we do not need to find the station point but can lay off this distance directly on the horizon.

True scale in 45° construction
1. Draw a horizon.
2. Lay off two vanishing points and bisect the distance between them to locate the diagonal vanishing point.
3. Divide the distance from the diagonal vanishing point to one vanishing point into units to equal the distance of the station point.
4. Draw the vertical measuring line and either project the units at 45° from the horizon or step them off on the measuring line to find the top and bottom of the cube.
5. Construct the diagonal plane of the cube to one side of *VML*.
6. Draw a diagonal from the lower far corner *D2* to the opposite vanishing point, locating the depth of the cube *X*. Complete the cube.

True scale in 30-60° construction
In 30-60° construction the station point is similarly related to the vanishing points.
1. Establish the unit measure on the horizon from the *VML* to the nearest *VP* and project it down 60° to the vertical measuring line to find the height of the cube.
2. Divide the horizon in the usual way to find measuring points and complete the cube.

True scale in parallel construction
In parallel construction, as in 45° construction, the unit is the same on the horizon as it is on the vertical measuring line.
When the face has been completed, the depth is found by drawing the diagonal to *DVP*.

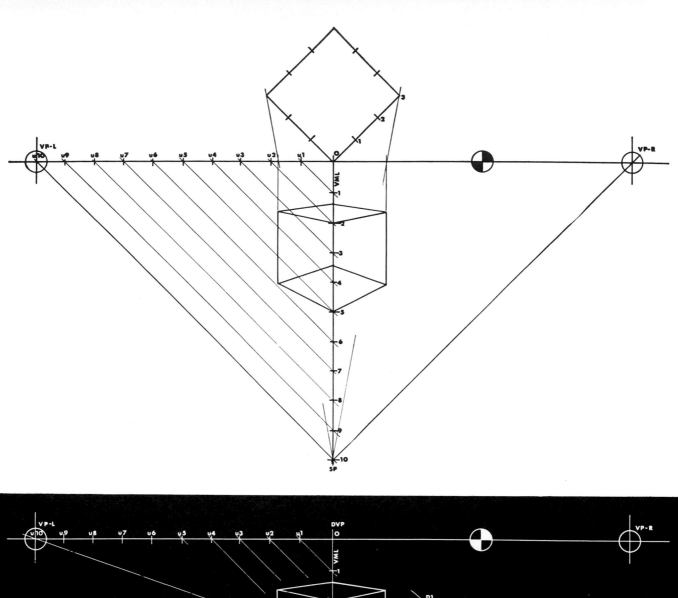
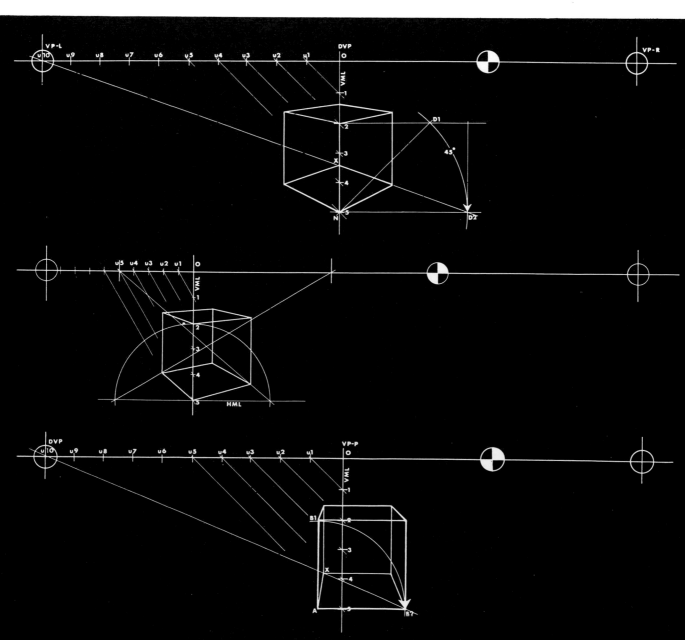

Scales for direct drawing

The artist who has to make a number of drawings using the same view and the same distance between the vanishing points can save a little time on original construction by using a perspective scale. Essentially, such scales use divisions of the horizon as a measure of fore-shortening. They are easy to make in any size and view, and a set of them can be a handy tool. I do not recommend their use by anyone who does not understand perspective drawing.

To make one of these scales, construct a horizon and mark off two vanishing points an even number of units apart. Construct a four-unit cube with its nearest angle close to ninety degrees and multiply it to make a vista of one-unit squares. Place a strip of paper along the horizon and project the intersections of the squares up to it, numbering them to the right and left from zero at the vertical measuring line. Note the unit distance to the vanishing points at the top of the scale.

To use the scale, draw a horizon and place the scale on it. Locate the vertical measuring line and the vanishing points as indicated on the scale. Mark off the true height of the object on the vertical measuring line; then project its depth down from the scale.

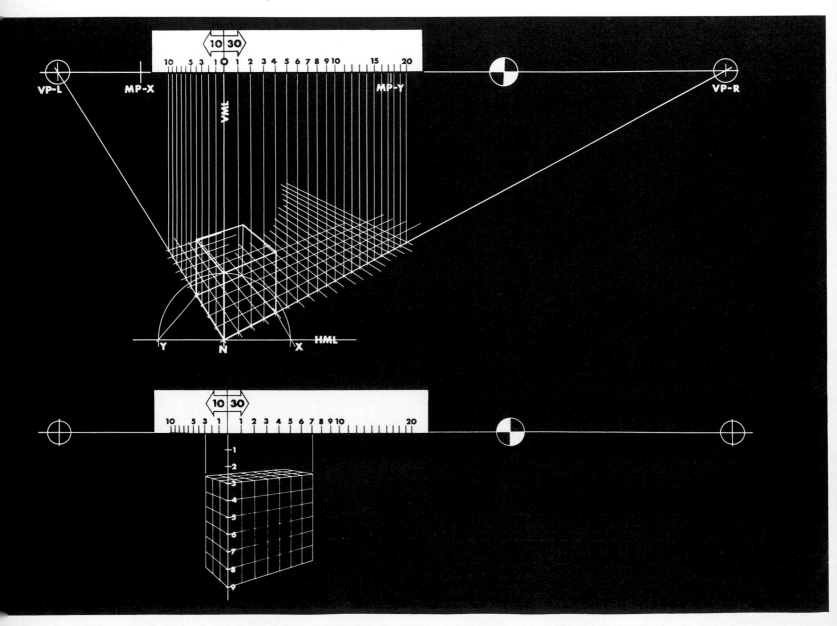

The lineaid

With ordinary perspective systems the lineaid is difficult to use, but with the system presented here it is very valuable, making it easy to construct a perspective view with one of the vanishing points off the table. In other words, it allows us to use an ordinary drawing board for perspective views that would ordinarily require a tremendous drawing area.

The lineaid is a long straight-edge ending in two moveable arms that can be fastened in any position. If the arms are placed against two pins set in the board, the lineaid will move up and down the board in a regular arc. The vanishing point is at the center of this arc; its position depends on the position of the arms. When the arms are at right angles to the blade, the vanishing point is at an infinite distance, and the lineaid is, in effect, a T-square. As the arms are turned, the vanishing point comes closer.

Suppose we wish to draw a 30-60° cube with one vanishing point off the table. First draw a horizon. Set the arms of the lineaid at the proper angle to give the desired distance between the vanishing points (this is not hard to judge by eye) and place two pins in the board (*x* and *y*) to hold them. Make sure that the lineaid lines up with the horizon, then rotate it down to the bottom of the drawing. Drive one pin in the left vanishing point and another against the lineaid at *z*. Stretch a string from these two pins and line it up with the lineaid and the horizon; the second vanishing point (*VP-R*) will be found at the apex of the string. Now divide the distance between the vanishing points with a steel tape or simply by folding the string to find the measuring points and the vertical measuring line. Since the lineaid supplies the right-hand perspective lines, we have no further need for *VP-R*.

The lineaid is particularly useful for three-point perspective, making it possible to draw a 45° cube with all three vanishing points off the table. As the illustration shows, three pairs of pins are set in a circle to provide three positions for the lineaid.

Other vanishing point tricks

In addition to the lineaid there are various home-made devices for drawing with one vanishing point off the board:

1. Cut an arc out of plastic or cardboard; fasten the inside piece to back of the T-square. Fasten the outside piece to the drawing board, taking care that its center falls on the horizon. These can be made in different sizes with their center distances noted.

2. Clamp a piece of wood to the table to hold the second vanishing point. Drive a pin into each vanishing point and stretch a wire or tough string between them, fastening the wire at one end by means of a light spring or rubber band. If a stiff enough wire is used, sketching can be done directly against it.

Special machines for drawing in perspective are interesting theoretically but usually very expensive and not much more useful than a straight-edge. I believe that the perspective system I have described makes complex equipment and special charts unnecessary.

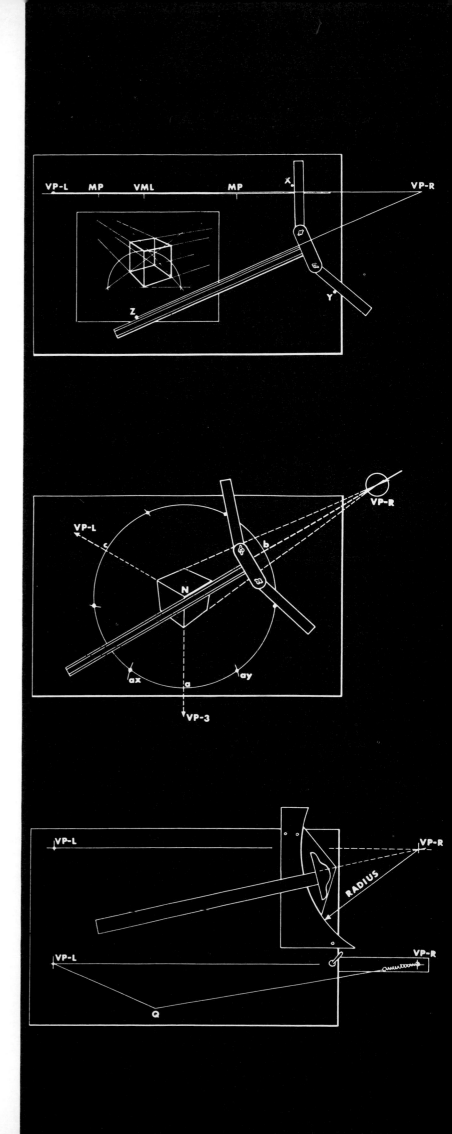

editorial associate: Deborah Allen
layout, cover and jacket: Rolf Strub
printing: Kingsport Press, Inc.